This book is a gift

To

_____

From

_____

Date

_____

Bible Promises to Bless Your Heart

Published by Christian Art Publishers,
PO Box 1599, Vereeniging, 1930, RSA

© 2017
First edition 2017

Designed by Christian Art Publishers

Images used under license from Shutterstock.com

Scripture quotations marked NIV are taken from the Holy Bible, New International Version® NIV®. Copyright © 1973, 1978, 1984, 2011 by International Bible Society. Used by permission of Zondervan Publishing House. All rights reserved.

Scripture quotations marked NLT are taken from the Holy Bible, New Living Translation®. Copyright © 1996, 2004, 2007 by Tyndale House Publishers, Inc., Carol Stream, Illinois 60188. All rights reserved.

Scripture quotations marked ESV are taken from the Holy Bible, English Standard Version. Copyright © 2001 by Crossway Bibles, a division of Good News Publishers. Used by permission. All rights reserved.

Scripture quotations marked CEV are taken from the Contemporary English Version®. Copyright © 1995 by American Bible Society. All rights reserved.

Printed in China

ISBN 978-1-4321-1621-7

Christian Art Publishers has made every effort to trace the ownership of all quotes and poems in this book. In the event of any questions that may arise from the use of any quote or poem, we regret any error made and will be pleased to make the necessary correction in future editions of this book.

18 19 20 21 22 23 24 25 26 27 – 14 13 12 11 10 9 8 7 6 5

BIBLE
Promises
TO *Bless*
YOUR HEART

CHRISTIAN ART
PUBLISHERS

Introduction

God's love and grace surround us
every moment of the day, wherever we are.
No matter what our circumstances,
God is always there for us.
365 Bible Promises to Bless Your Heart
will remind you of this wonderful
assurance every day of the year.
Every month focuses on a different
aspect of God's love and every Scripture verse is
accompanied by an inspirational quote.
As you ponder on these promises,
be joyful in the knowledge that you
are important to God and that
He loves you unconditionally.

January

God will love, care and
comfort you always.

I am like an olive tree growing in God's house,
and I can count on His love forever and ever.

Ps. 52:8 CEV

The LORD your God goes with you,
He will never leave you nor forsake you.

Deut. 31:6 NIV

"I am the LORD your God who takes hold
of your right hand and says to you,
Do not fear; I will help you."

Isa. 41:13 NIV

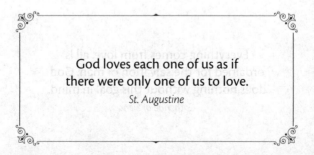

God loves each one of us as if
there were only one of us to love.

St. Augustine

The LORD is good! His love and
faithfulness will last forever.
Ps. 100:5 CEV

Give thanks to the LORD, for He is good!
His faithful love endures forever.
Ps. 106:1 NLT

The LORD will watch over your coming
and going both now and forevermore.
Ps. 121:8 NIV

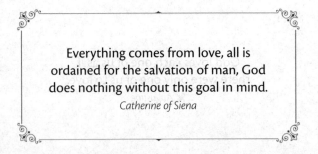

Everything comes from love, all is
ordained for the salvation of man, God
does nothing without this goal in mind.

Catherine of Siena

Your steadfast love, O LORD, extends to the
heavens, Your faithfulness to the clouds.
Ps. 36:5 ESV

I find true comfort, LORD, because
Your laws have stood the test of time.
Ps. 119:52 CEV

The grass withers and the flowers fall,
but the word of our God endures forever.
Isa. 40:8 NIV

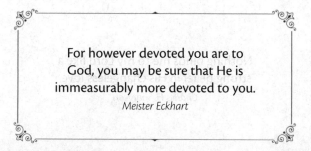

For however devoted you are to
God, you may be sure that He is
immeasurably more devoted to you.
Meister Eckhart

*This is how we know what love is: Jesus Christ
laid down His life for us. And we ought to lay
down our lives for our brothers and sisters.*

1 John 3:16 NIV

*"For God so loved the world, that He gave
His only Son, that whoever believes in
Him should not perish but have eternal life."*

John 3:16 ESV

*"Love your enemies! Do good to them. Lend to them
without expecting to be repaid. Then your reward
from heaven will be very great, and you will truly
be acting as children of the Most High, for He
is kind to those who are unthankful and wicked."*

Luke 6:35 NLT

Nothing binds me to my Lord like a
strong belief in His changeless love.

Charles H. Spurgeon

This is real love – not that we loved God,
but that He loved us and sent His Son
as a sacrifice to take away our sins.

1 John 4:10 NLT

But God demonstrates His own love for us in this:
While we were still sinners, Christ died for us.

Rom. 5:8 NIV

God was merciful! We were dead because of our sins,
but God loved us so much that He made us alive with
Christ, and God's wonderful kindness is what saves you.

Eph. 2:4-5 CEV

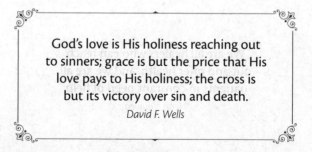

God's love is His holiness reaching out
to sinners; grace is but the price that His
love pays to His holiness; the cross is
but its victory over sin and death.

David F. Wells

*God heals the brokenhearted
and binds up their wounds.*

Ps. 147:3 NIV

*"Blessed are those who mourn,
for they shall be comforted."*

Matt. 5:4 ESV

*I will be glad and rejoice in Your unfailing
love, for You have seen my troubles, and
You care about the anguish of my soul.*

Ps. 31:7 NLT

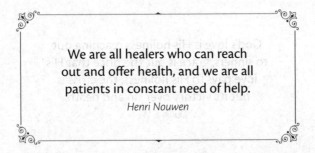

We are all healers who can reach
out and offer health, and we are all
patients in constant need of help.

Henri Nouwen

*Praise God, the Father of our Lord Jesus Christ! The Father
is a merciful God, who always gives us comfort. He
comforts us when we are in trouble, so that we can
share that same comfort with others in trouble.*

2 Cor. 1:3-4 CEV

*Cast your cares on the LORD and He will sustain
you; He will never let the righteous be shaken.*

Ps. 55:22 NIV

*"I will turn their mourning into joy.
I will comfort them and exchange
their sorrow for rejoicing."*

Jer. 31:13 NLT

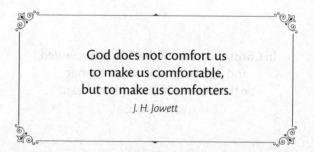

God does not comfort us
to make us comfortable,
but to make us comforters.

J. H. Jowett

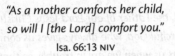

"As a mother comforts her child,
so will I [the Lord] comfort you."

Isa. 66:13 NIV

"I will still be the same when you are old and gray,
and I will take care of you. I created you.
I will carry you and always keep you safe."

Isa. 46:4 CEV

In His kindness God called you to share in
His eternal glory by means of Christ Jesus.
So after you have suffered a little while,
He will restore, support, and strengthen you,
and He will place you on a firm foundation.

1 Pet. 5:10 NLT

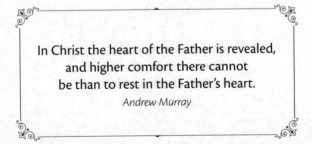

In Christ the heart of the Father is revealed,
and higher comfort there cannot
be than to rest in the Father's heart.

Andrew Murray

*The LORD comforts His people and will
have compassion on His afflicted ones.*
Isa. 49:13 NIV

*The LORD is a mighty tower where
His people can run for safety.*
Prov. 18:10 CEV

*He will again have compassion on us; He will
tread our iniquities underfoot. You will
cast all our sins into the depths of the sea.*
Mic. 7:19 ESV

No affliction nor temptation, no guilt
nor power of sin, no wounded spirit nor
terrified conscience, should induce us to
despair of help and comfort from God!

Thomas Scott

The LORD will bring comfort.

Isa. 51:3 CEV

The LORD remembers us and will bless us.

Ps. 115:12 NIV

Even if my father and mother abandon me,
the LORD will hold me close.

Ps. 27:10 NLT

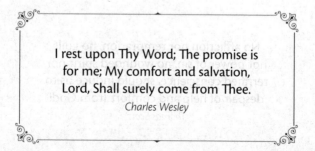

I rest upon Thy Word; The promise is
for me; My comfort and salvation,
Lord, Shall surely come from Thee.

Charles Wesley

You will increase my greatness
and comfort me again.

Ps. 71:21 ESV

"I, yes I, am the One who comforts
you. So why are you afraid?"

Isa. 51:12 NLT

In times of trouble, You will protect me.
You will hide me in Your tent and
keep me safe on top of a mighty rock.

Ps. 27:5 CEV

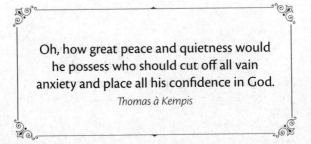

Oh, how great peace and quietness would
he possess who should cut off all vain
anxiety and place all his confidence in God.

Thomas à Kempis

I trust You, Lord. I celebrate and shout
because You are kind. You saw all
my suffering, and You cared for me.
Ps. 31:6-7 CEV

Praise the Lord, all nations! Extol Him, all peoples!
For great is His steadfast love toward us, and
the faithfulness of the Lord endures forever.
Praise the Lord!
Ps. 117:1-2 ESV

But each day the Lord pours His
unfailing love upon me, and
through each night I sing His songs,
praying to God who gives me life.
Ps. 42:8 NLT

God, who foresaw your tribulation, has
specially armed you to go through it,
not without pain but without stain.

C. S. Lewis

*"If God cares so wonderfully for flowers that
are here today and thrown into the fire
tomorrow, He will certainly care for you."*

Luke 12:28 NLT

*"Though the mountains be shaken
and the hills be removed, yet My
unfailing love for you will not be shaken
nor My covenant of peace be removed."*

Isa. 54:10 NIV

*"I will be with you always,
even until the end of the world."*

Matt. 28:20 CEV

Just as the body wears clothes and the
flesh skin, and the bones flesh, and the heart
the chest, so we, soul and body are clothed
and enfolded in the goodness of God.

Julian of Norwich

*Cast all your anxiety on Him
because He cares for you.*

1 Pet. 5:7 NIV

*"Come to me, all who labor and are
heavy laden, and I will give you rest."*

Matt. 11:28 ESV

LORD, *You alone are my portion and
my cup; You make my lot secure.*

Ps. 16:5 NIV

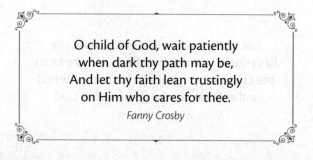

O child of God, wait patiently
when dark thy path may be,
And let thy faith lean trustingly
on Him who cares for thee.

Fanny Crosby

Though the LORD is great,
He cares for the humble.

Ps. 138:6 NLT

The LORD is disgusted with all who do wrong,
but He loves everyone who does right.

Prov. 15:9 CEV

The LORD remembers us and will bless us.

Ps. 115:12 NIV

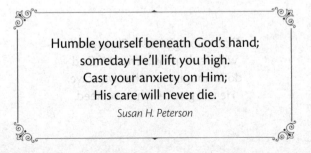

Humble yourself beneath God's hand;
someday He'll lift you high.
Cast your anxiety on Him;
His care will never die.

Susan H. Peterson

The LORD cares for His nation,
just as shepherds care for their flocks.
Isa. 40:11 CEV

What is mankind that You are mindful of them,
human beings that You care for them.
Ps. 8:4 NIV

He will not let your foot be moved;
He who keeps you will not slumber.
Ps. 121:3 ESV

Doth God give us a Christ, and
will He deny us a crust? If God
doth not give us what we crave,
He will give us what we need.

Thomas Watson

*The Lord cares for the helpless. He does
not ignore the cries of those who suffer.*

Ps. 9:11-12 NLT

*Let Your unfailing love comfort me,
just as You promised me.*

Ps. 119:76 NLT

The LORD will love you and bless you.

Deut. 7:13 CEV

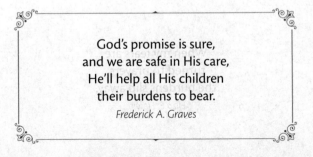

God's promise is sure,
and we are safe in His care,
He'll help all His children
their burdens to bear.

Frederick A. Graves

*"I am the One who answers
your prayers and cares for you."*
Hos. 14:8 NLT

*Surely the righteous will never be shaken;
they will be remembered forever.
They will have no fear of bad news;
their hearts are steadfast, trusting in the LORD.*
Ps. 112:6-7 NLT

*But You, O Lord, are a God merciful and
gracious, slow to anger and abounding
in steadfast love and faithfulness.*
Ps. 86:15 ESV

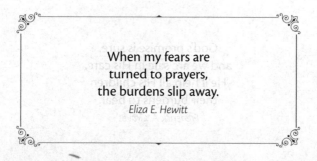

When my fears are
turned to prayers,
the burdens slip away.
Eliza E. Hewitt

As we share abundantly in Christ's sufferings, so
through Christ we share abundantly in comfort too.
2 Cor. 1:5 ESV

"I lavish unfailing love for a thousand generations
on those who love Me and obey My commands."
Deut. 5:10 NLT

As a father has compassion on His children,
so the LORD has compassion on those who fear Him.
Ps. 103:13 NIV

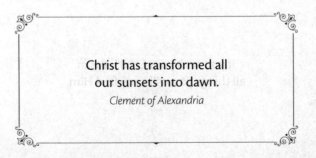

Christ has transformed all
our sunsets into dawn.
Clement of Alexandria

The hand of our God is for good
on all who seek Him.
Ezra 8:22 ESV

The LORD is good, a strong refuge when trouble
comes. He is close to those who trust in Him.
Nah. 1:7 NLT

The Lord is good to everyone. He showers
compassion on all His creation.
Ps. 145:9 NLT

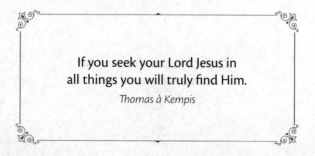

If you seek your Lord Jesus in
all things you will truly find Him.

Thomas à Kempis

God showed how much He loved us by sending
His one and only Son into the world so
that we might have eternal life through Him.

1 John 4:9 NLT

"As the Father has loved Me,
so have I loved you. Abide in My love."

John 15:9 ESV

Hope does not put us to shame, because
God's love has been poured out into
our hearts through the Holy Spirit,
who has been given to us.

Rom. 5:5 NIV

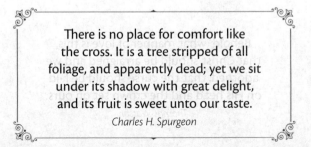

There is no place for comfort like
the cross. It is a tree stripped of all
foliage, and apparently dead; yet we sit
under its shadow with great delight,
and its fruit is sweet unto our taste.

Charles H. Spurgeon

Jesus treated us much better than we deserve.
He made us acceptable to God and
gave us the hope of eternal life.

Titus 3:7 CEV

"And the very hairs on your head are all numbered.
So don't be afraid; you are more valuable
to God than a whole flock of sparrows."

Matt. 10:30-31 NLT

"I will rejoice in doing them good, and I
will plant them in this land in faithfulness,
with all My heart and all My soul."

Jer. 32:41 ESV

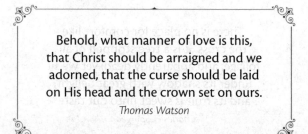

Behold, what manner of love is this,
that Christ should be arraigned and we
adorned, that the curse should be laid
on His head and the crown set on ours.

Thomas Watson

"I will heal you and love you without limit."
Hos. 14:4 CEV

So now faith, hope, and love abide,
these three; but the greatest of these is love.
1 Cor. 13:13 ESV

Give thanks to the God of gods.
His love endures forever.
Ps. 136:2 NIV

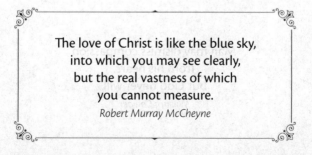

The love of Christ is like the blue sky,
into which you may see clearly,
but the real vastness of which
you cannot measure.

Robert Murray McCheyne

*Because of the LORD's great love we are not
consumed, for His compassions never fail. They
are new every morning; great is Your faithfulness.*

Lam. 3:22-23 NIV

*God is our refuge and strength,
a very present help in trouble.*

Ps. 46:1 ESV

*The Lord is faithful; He will strengthen
you and guard you from the evil one.*

2 Thess. 3:3 NLT

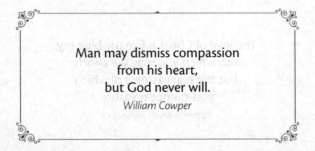

Man may dismiss compassion
from his heart,
but God never will.

William Cowper

"I will comfort those who mourn," says the LORD.

Isa. 57:18-19 NLT

The LORD is a refuge for the oppressed,
a stronghold in times of trouble.

Ps. 9:9 NIV

"He will wipe away every tear from their
eyes, and death shall be no more,
neither shall there be mourning,
nor crying, nor pain anymore, for
the former things have passed away."

Rev. 21:4 ESV

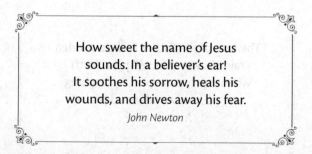

How sweet the name of Jesus
sounds. In a believer's ear!
It soothes his sorrow, heals his
wounds, and drives away his fear.

John Newton

*"I care about you and I will
pay attention to you."*

Ezek. 36:9 NLT

Your Father knows what you need before you ask Him.

Matt. 6:8 NIV

*Love the LORD your God, and serve Him
with all your heart and with all your soul,
He will give the rain for your land in its
season, the early rain and the later rain,
that you may gather in your grain and
your wine and your oil. And He will
give grass in your fields for your livestock,
and you shall eat and be full.*

Deut. 11:13-15 ESV

The love of the Father is like a sudden
rain shower that will pour forth
when you least expect it, catching
you up into wonder and praise.

Richard J. Foster

*God's love can always be trusted, and His
faithfulness lasts as long as the heavens.*

Ps. 89:2 CEV

*How priceless is Your unfailing love, O God!
People take refuge in the shadow of Your wings.*

Ps. 36:7 NIV

*May God's grace be eternally upon
all who love our Lord Jesus Christ.*

Eph. 6:24 NLT

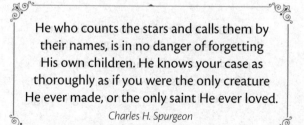

He who counts the stars and calls them by
their names, is in no danger of forgetting
His own children. He knows your case as
thoroughly as if you were the only creature
He ever made, or the only saint He ever loved.

Charles H. Spurgeon

God's love and kindness will shine upon
us like the sun that rises in the sky.

Luke 1:78 CEV

May you experience the love of Christ,
though it is too great to understand fully.
Then you will be made complete with all the
fullness of life and power that comes from God.

Eph. 3:19 NLT

"What no eye has seen, nor ear heard,
nor the heart of man imagined, what
God has prepared for those who love Him."

1 Cor. 2:9 ESV

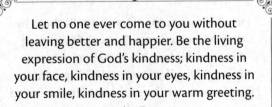

Let no one ever come to you without
leaving better and happier. Be the living
expression of God's kindness; kindness in
your face, kindness in your eyes, kindness in
your smile, kindness in your warm greeting.

Mother Teresa

Nothing can ever separate us from God's love.
Rom. 8:38 NLT

"For the Father Himself loves you,
because you have loved Me and
have believed that I came from God."
John 16:27 ESV

"I am one with them, and You are one with Me,
so that they may become completely one.
Then this world's people will know that
You sent Me. They will know that You love
My followers as much as You love Me."
John 17:23 CEV

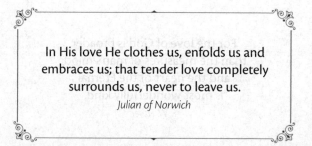

In His love He clothes us, enfolds us and
embraces us; that tender love completely
surrounds us, never to leave us.

Julian of Norwich

See how very much our Father loves us, for He
calls us His children, and that is what we are!

1 John 3:1 NLT

"*I will make you My wife forever,*
showing you righteousness and justice,
unfailing love and compassion. I will be
faithful to you and make you Mine,
and you will finally know me as the LORD."

Hos. 2:19-20 NLT

"*Can a woman forget her nursing child,*
that she should have no compassion
on the son of her womb? Even these
may forget, yet I will not forget you."

Isa. 49:15 ESV

For the love of God is broader
than the measures of man's mind;
and the heart of the Eternal
is most wonderfully kind.

F. W. Faber

Only God works great miracles.
God's love never fails.

Ps. 136:4 CEV

He gives justice to the oppressed and food to the
hungry. The LORD opens the eyes of the blind.
The LORD lifts up those who are weighed down.

Ps. 146:7-8 NLT

"I made known to them Your name,
and I will continue to make it known,
that the love with which You have
loved Me may be in them, and I in them."

John 17:26 ESV

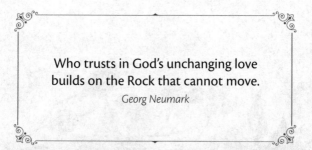

Who trusts in God's unchanging love
builds on the Rock that cannot move.

Georg Neumark

February

*God will protect you
and provide for you.*

God will meet all your needs according
to the riches of His glory in Christ Jesus.

Phil. 4:19 NIV

I am the LORD your God. Just ask,
and I will give you whatever you need.

Ps. 81:10 CEV

God's way is perfect. All the LORD's promises prove true.
He is a shield for all who look to Him for protection.

Ps. 18:30 NLT

God will not lightly or easily lose His people.
He has provided well for us: blood to wash
us in; a Priest to pray for us, that we may be
made to persevere; and, in case we foully
fall, an Advocate to plead our cause.

John Bunyan

*God can bless you with everything you need,
and you will always have more than enough
to do all kinds of good things for others.*

2 Cor. 9:8 CEV

"Keep on asking, and you will receive what you ask for."

Matt. 7:7 NLT

*You care for the land and water it; You enrich
it abundantly. The streams of God are
filled with water to provide the people
with grain, for so You have ordained it.*

Ps. 65:9 NIV

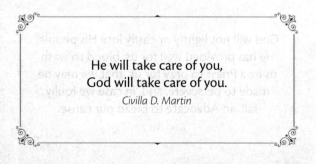

He will take care of you,
God will take care of you.

Civilla D. Martin

*His divine power has given us everything we
need for a godly life through our knowledge of
Him who called us by His own glory and goodness.*

2 Pet. 1:3 NIV

*"I tell you, do not be anxious about your life,
what you will eat or what you will drink,
nor about your body, what you will
put on. Is not life more than food,
and the body more than clothing?"*

Matt. 6:25 ESV

*"By My power I will make My people strong, and by
My authority" they will go wherever they wish.*

Zech. 10:12 NLT

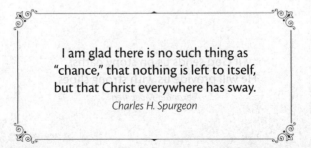

I am glad there is no such thing as
"chance," that nothing is left to itself,
but that Christ everywhere has sway.

Charles H. Spurgeon

*"Your Father knows what you
need before you ask Him."*

Matt. 6:8 ESV

*"You will be blessed in the city
and blessed in the country."*

Deut. 28:3 NIV

"For I know the plans I have for you," says
the LORD. *"They are plans for good and not
for disaster, to give you a future and a hope."*

Jer. 29:11 NLT

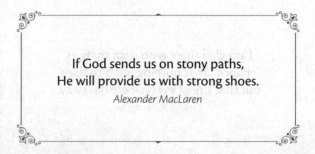

If God sends us on stony paths,
He will provide us with strong shoes.

Alexander MacLaren

FEBRUARY 5

The Lord is my Shepherd, I lack nothing.
He makes me lie down in green pastures,
He leads me beside quiet waters.

Ps. 23:1-2 NIV

The Lord does not let the
righteous go hungry.

Prov. 10:3 ESV

You are my hiding place!
You protect me from trouble.

Ps. 32:7 CEV

A firm faith in the universal providence of God is the solution of all earthly problems.

B. B. Warfield

He will send the rains in their proper seasons –
the early and late rains – so you can
bring in your harvests of grain, new wine,
and olive oil. He will give you lush
pastureland for your livestock, and you
yourselves will have all you want to eat.

Deut. 11:14 -15 NLT

He makes grass grow for the cattle, and plants for
people to cultivate – bringing forth food from the earth.

Ps. 104:14 NIV

For the LORD God is our sun and our shield. He
gives us grace and glory. The LORD will withhold
no good thing from those who do what is right.

Ps. 84:11 NLT

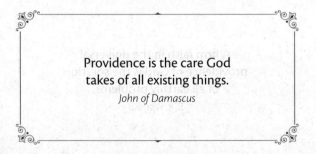

Providence is the care God
takes of all existing things.
John of Damascus

*The LORD will protect you and keep you
safe from all dangers. The LORD will protect
you now and always wherever you go.*

Ps. 121:7-8 CEV

*The LORD is my rock, my fortress, and my Savior;
my God is my rock, in whom I find protection.
He is my shield, the power that saves me, and
my place of safety. He is my refuge, my Savior,
the one who saves me from violence.*

2 Sam. 22:2-3 NLT

*Fear not, stand firm, and see the salvation of the
LORD, which He will work for you today. The LORD
will fight for you, and you have only to be silent.*

Exod. 14:13-14 ESV

When we stray from His presence, He longs
for you to come back. He weeps that you are
missing out on His love, protection and provision.
He throws His arms open, runs toward you,
gathers you up, and welcomes you home.

Charles Stanley

The name of the LORD is a fortified tower;
the righteous run to it and are safe.

Prov. 18:10 NIV

Protect me, LORD God! I run to You for safety.

Ps. 16:1 CEV

"All who listen to me will live in peace,
untroubled by fear of harm."

Prov. 1:33 NLT

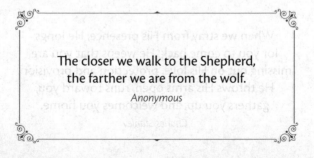

The closer we walk to the Shepherd,
the farther we are from the wolf.
Anonymous

*The Lord is faithful, and He will strengthen
you and protect you from the evil one.*
2 Thess. 3:3 NIV

*My enemies will retreat when I call to You
for help. This I know: God is on my side!*
Ps. 56:9 NLT

*The Lord will rescue me from every evil deed and
bring me safely into His heavenly kingdom.*
2 Tim. 4:18 ESV

Let God's promises shine
on your problems.

Corrie ten Boom

The LORD is my fortress, protecting me
from danger, so why should I tremble?
Ps. 27:1 NLT

"When you are in trouble, call out to Me. I will
answer and be there to protect and honor you."
Ps. 91:15 CEV

For in the day of trouble He will
keep me safe in His dwelling.
Ps. 27:5 NIV

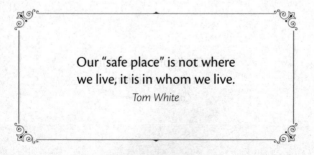

Our "safe place" is not where
we live, it is in whom we live.
Tom White

You are my fortress, my place of safety;
You are my God, and I trust You.

Ps. 91:2 CEV

Be to me a rock of refuge, to which I may
continually come; You have given the command
to save me, for You are my rock and my fortress.

Ps. 71:3 ESV

Having hope will give you courage. You
will be protected and will rest in safety.

Job 11:18 NLT

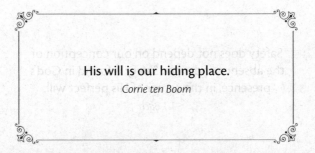

His will is our hiding place.
Corrie ten Boom

The LORD will be your confidence and
will keep your foot from being caught.
Prov. 3:26 ESV

Who is going to harm you if
you are eager to do good?
1 Pet. 3:13 NIV

The LORD Most High loves you ... He will
live among your hills and protect you.
Deut. 33:12 CEV

Safety does not depend on our conception of
the absence of danger. Safety is found in God's
presence, in the center of His perfect will.

T. J. Bach

"Be strong and courageous. Do not be frightened,
and do not be dismayed, for the LORD
your God is with you wherever you go."

Josh. 1:9 ESV

The LORD Most High is your fortress. Run to Him for
safety, and no terrible disasters will strike you. God will
command His angels to protect you wherever you go.

Ps. 91:9-11 CEV

It is impossible to please God without faith. Anyone
who wants to come to Him must believe that God exists
and that He rewards those who sincerely seek Him.

Heb. 11:6 NLT

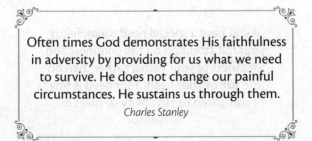

Often times God demonstrates His faithfulness
in adversity by providing for us what we need
to survive. He does not change our painful
circumstances. He sustains us through them.

Charles Stanley

The LORD your God will personally go ahead of you.
He will neither fail you nor abandon you.

Deut. 31:6 NLT

You are God's chosen and special people.
You are a group of royal priests and a holy
nation. God has brought you out of
darkness into His marvelous light.

1 Pet. 2:9 CEV

In Him we were also chosen, having been
predestined according to the plan of
Him who works out everything in
conformity with the purpose of His will.

Eph. 1:11 NIV

If you have a special need today, focus
your full attention on the goodness and
greatness of your Father rather than on
the size of your need. Your need is tiny
compared to His ability to meet it.

Bill Patterson

"Fear not, for I am with you; be not dismayed,
for I am your God; I will strengthen you,
I will help you, I will uphold you."

Isa. 41:10 ESV

The LORD gives His people strength.
The LORD blesses them with peace.

Ps. 29:11 NLT

God always does what He plans, and that's
why He appointed Christ to choose us.

Ps. 5:12 CEV

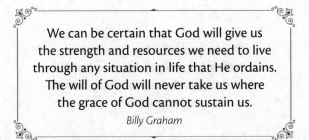

We can be certain that God will give us
the strength and resources we need to live
through any situation in life that He ordains.
The will of God will never take us where
the grace of God cannot sustain us.

Billy Graham

The LORD is on my side; I will not fear.
What can man do to me?
Ps. 118:6 ESV

They do not fear bad news; they confidently
trust the LORD to care for them.
Ps. 112:7 NLT

You will laugh at the threat of destruction and
famine. And you won't be afraid of wild animals.
Job 5:22 CEV

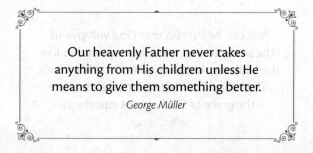

Our heavenly Father never takes
anything from His children unless He
means to give them something better.
George Müller

"*I am the* L<small>ORD</small> *your God who takes hold of your right hand and says to you, Do not fear; I will help you.*"

Isa. 41:13 NIV

"*A thousand may fall at your side, ten thousand at your right hand, but it will not come near you.*"

Ps. 91:7 ESV

"*I brought you here to my land, where food is abundant.*"

Jer. 2:7 CEV

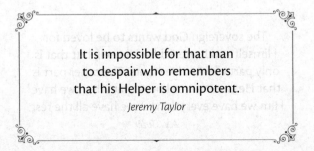

It is impossible for that man to despair who remembers that his Helper is omnipotent.

Jeremy Taylor

"Seek the Kingdom of God above all else,
and He will give you everything you need."
Luke 12:31 NLT

If you respect the LORD, you and your
children have a strong fortress.
Prov. 14:26 CEV

Taste and see that the LORD is good.
Oh, the joys of those who take refuge in Him!
Ps. 34:8 NLT

The sovereign God wants to be loved for
Himself and honored for Himself, but that is
only part of what He wants. The other part is
that He wants us to know that when we have
Him we have everything – we have all the rest.

A.W. Tozer

*Love the LORD, all you godly ones! For the
LORD protects those who are loyal to Him.*

Ps. 31:23 NLT

*If you honor the LORD, His angel will protect you.
Discover for yourself that the LORD is kind.
Come to Him for protection, and you will be glad.*

Ps. 34:7-8 CEV

*Though I walk in the midst of trouble, You preserve
my life. You stretch out Your hand against the anger
of my foes; with Your right hand You save me.*

Ps. 138:7 NIV

Commit every particle of your being in all
things, down to the smallest details of your
life, eagerly and with perfect trust to the
unfailing and most sure providence of God.

Jean-Pierre de Caussade

He grants a treasure of common sense to the honest.
He is a shield to those who walk with integrity.

Prov. 2:7 NLT

Young lions may go hungry or even starve, but if you trust
the LORD, you will never miss out on anything good.

Ps. 34:10 CEV

Let all who take refuge in You rejoice; let them ever
sing for joy, and spread Your protection over them,
that those who love Your name may exult in You.

Ps. 5:11 ESV

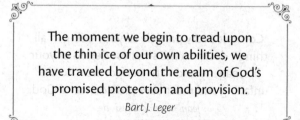

The moment we begin to tread upon
the thin ice of our own abilities, we
have traveled beyond the realm of God's
promised protection and provision.

Bart J. Leger

We know that everyone who has been born of God does not keep on sinning, but He who was born of God protects him, and the evil one does not touch him.
1 John 5:18 ESV

Children, you belong to God, and you have defeated these enemies. God's Spirit is in you and is more powerful than the one that is in the world.
1 John 4:4 CEV

Oh, the joys of those who are kind to the poor! The LORD rescues them when they are in trouble. The LORD protects them and keeps them alive. He gives them prosperity in the land and rescues them from their enemies.
Ps. 41:1-2 NLT

Bring Christ's Word – Christ's promise, and Christ's sacrifice – His blood, with thee, and not one of heaven's blessings can be denied thee.
Adam Clarke

God is the One who provides seed for the farmer
and then bread to eat. In the same way, He
will provide and increase your resources and
then produce a great harvest of generosity in you.
2 Cor. 9:10 NLT

"Every moving thing that lives shall be food for you.
And as I gave you the green plants, I give you everything."
Gen. 9:3 ESV

He gives food to His worshipers and
always keeps His agreement with them.
Ps. 111:5 CEV

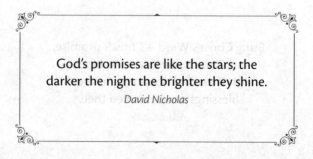

God's promises are like the stars; the
darker the night the brighter they shine.
David Nicholas

*If anyone serves, they should do so with the
strength God provides, so that in all things
God may be praised through Jesus Christ.*

1 Pet. 4:11 NIV

*"If they listen and obey God, they will be
blessed with prosperity throughout their
lives. All their years will be pleasant."*

Job 36:11 NLT

*May the God of peace Himself sanctify you completely,
and may your whole spirit and soul and
body be kept blameless at the coming of our
Lord Jesus Christ. He who calls you is faithful.*

1 Thess. 5:23-24 ESV

Our heavenly Father is a very experienced
One. He knows very well that His children wake
up with a good appetite every morning ... He
sustained 3 million Israelites in the wilderness
for 40 years ... Depend on it, God's work done
in God's way will never lack God's supply.

James Hudson Taylor

*No one is like the LORD! You protect
the helpless from those in power;
You save the poor and needy
from those who hurt them.*

Ps. 35:10 CEV

*May the LORD answer you when you are in distress;
may the name of the God of Jacob protect you.*

Ps. 20:1 NIV

*"I give them eternal life, and they will never perish,
and no one will snatch them out of My hand."*

John 10:28 ESV

We never know how much real faith we
have until it is put to the test in some fierce
storm; and that is the reason why the Savior
is on board. If you are ever to be strong
in the Lord and the power of His might,
your strength will be born in some storm.

Anonymous

It is good for me to be near You.
I choose You as my protector, and
I will tell about Your wonderful deeds.

Ps. 73:28 CEV

Who will protect me from the wicked? Who will stand up
for me against evildoers? Unless the LORD had helped me,
I would soon have settled in the silence of the grave.

Ps. 94:16-17 NLT

And I will do whatever you ask in My name,
so that the Father may be glorified in the Son.
You may ask Me for anything in My name,
and I will do it.

John 14:13-14 NIV

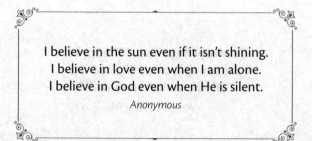

I believe in the sun even if it isn't shining.
I believe in love even when I am alone.
I believe in God even when He is silent.

Anonymous

*God will protect you from harm, no
matter how often trouble may strike.*

Job 5:19 CEV

*God is our refuge and strength,
an ever-present help in trouble.*

Ps. 46:1 NIV

*"No weapon that is fashioned against you shall succeed,
and you shall refute every tongue that rises against you
in judgment. This is the heritage of the servants of the
LORD and their vindication from Me," declares the LORD.*

Isa. 54:17 ESV

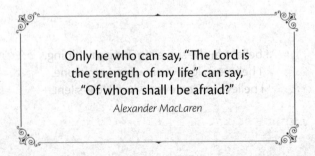

Only he who can say, "The Lord is
the strength of my life" can say,
"Of whom shall I be afraid?"

Alexander MacLaren

*"Because the poor are plundered and the
needy groan, I will now arise," says the Lord.
"I will protect them from those who malign them."*
Ps. 12:5 NIV

*O Lord, keep me out of the hands of the
wicked. Protect me from those who are
violent, for they are plotting against me.*
Ps. 140:4 NLT

*Our Lord and our God, You are like the sun and also
like a shield. You treat us with kindness and with honor,
never denying any good thing to those who live right.*
Ps. 84:11 CEV

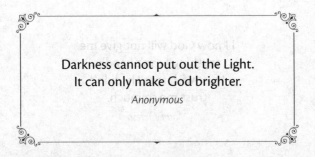

**Darkness cannot put out the Light.
It can only make God brighter.**

Anonymous

Even when I walk through the darkest valley,
I will not be afraid, for You are close beside me.
Your rod and Your staff protect and comfort me.

Ps. 23:4 NLT

In peace I will both lie down and sleep; for
You alone, O LORD, make me dwell in safety.

Ps. 4:8 ESV

"When you cross deep rivers, I will
be with you and you won't drown.
When you walk through fire, you won't
be burned or scorched by the flames."

Isa. 43:2 CEV

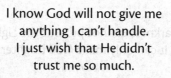

I know God will not give me
anything I can't handle.
I just wish that He didn't
trust me so much.

Mother Teresa

March

*God will give you peace,
rest and eternal life.*

God will are you better,
rest and cereal life

"I give you peace, the kind of peace that only I can give. It isn't like the peace that this world can give. So don't be worried or afraid."
John 14:27 CEV

In peace I will lie down and sleep, for You alone, O LORD, will keep me safe.
Ps. 4:8 NLT

The effect of righteousness will be peace, and the result of righteousness, quietness and trust forever.
Isa. 32:17 ESV

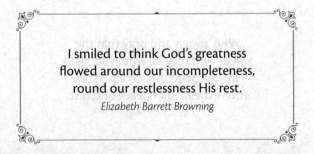

I smiled to think God's greatness flowed around our incompleteness, round our restlessness His rest.
Elizabeth Barrett Browning

The LORD gives perfect peace
to those whose faith is firm.

Isa. 26:3 CEV

"Your faith has saved you; go in peace."

Luke 7:50 ESV

There is a special rest still
waiting for the people of God.

Heb. 4:9 NLT

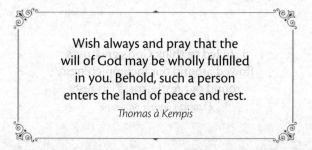

Wish always and pray that the
will of God may be wholly fulfilled
in you. Behold, such a person
enters the land of peace and rest.

Thomas à Kempis

*Those who love Your instructions have
great peace and do not stumble.*

Ps. 119:165 NLT

*Mark the blameless and behold the upright,
for there is a future for the man of peace.*

Ps. 37:37 ESV

*He will also keep you firm to the end, so that you will
be blameless on the day of our Lord Jesus Christ.*

1 Cor. 1:8 NIV

If God be our God, He will give us peace
in trouble. When there is a storm
without, He will make music within.
The world can create trouble in peace,
but God can create peace in trouble.

Thomas Watson

*May the Lord of peace Himself give you
His peace at all times and in every
situation. The Lord be with you all.*

2 Thess. 3:16 NLT

*Be still in the presence of the LORD, and
wait patiently for Him to act. Don't
worry about evil people who prosper
or fret about their wicked schemes.*

Ps. 37:7 NLT

*If possible, so far as it depends
on you, live peaceably with all.*

Rom. 12:18 ESV

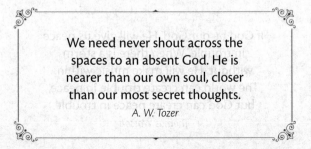

We need never shout across the
spaces to an absent God. He is
nearer than our own soul, closer
than our most secret thoughts.

A. W. Tozer

"In this place I will grant peace,"
declares the LORD Almighty.

Hag. 2:9 NIV

"God blesses those people who make peace.
They will be called His children!"

Matt. 5:9 CEV

"May the LORD show you His
favor and give you His peace."

Num. 6:26 NLT

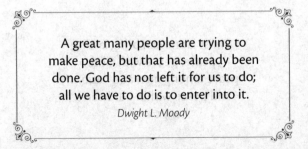

A great many people are trying to
make peace, but that has already been
done. God has not left it for us to do;
all we have to do is to enter into it.

Dwight L. Moody

To us a child is born, and He will be called
Wonderful Counselor, Mighty God,
Everlasting Father, Prince of Peace.

Isa. 9:6 NIV

"Be still, and know that I am God.
I will be exalted among the nations,
I will be exalted in the earth!"

Ps. 46:10 ESV

Those who feel tired and worn
out will find new life and energy.

Jer. 31:25 CEV

Christ alone can bring lasting
peace, peace with God,
peace among men and nations,
and peace within our hearts.

Billy Graham

The LORD said, "I will go with you and give you peace."

Exod. 33:14 CEV

He who dwells in the shelter of the Most High
will abide in the shadow of the Almighty.

Ps. 91:1 ESV

The fruit of that righteousness will be peace;
its effect will be quietness and confidence forever.

Isa. 32:17 NIV

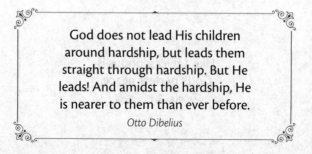

God does not lead His children
around hardship, but leads them
straight through hardship. But He
leads! And amidst the hardship, He
is nearer to them than ever before.

Otto Dibelius

*Do not be anxious about anything, but in everything
by prayer and supplication with thanksgiving let
your requests be made known to God. And the
peace of God, which surpasses all understanding,
will guard your hearts and your minds in Christ Jesus.*

Phil. 4:6-7 ESV

*Fear of the LORD leads to life, bringing
security and protection from harm.*

Prov. 19:23 NLT

*The LORD gives perfect peace to
those whose faith is firm.*

Isa. 26:3 CEV

Like a river glorious is
God's perfect peace.

Frances R. Havergal

*"Come to Me, all you who are weary and burdened,
and I will give you rest. Take My yoke upon you
and learn from Me, for I am gentle and humble
in heart, and you will find rest for your souls.
For My yoke is easy and My burden is light."*

Matt. 11:28-30 NIV

*"I have said these things to you, that in Me you may
have peace. In the world you will have tribulation.
But take heart; I have overcome the world."*

John 16:33 ESV

*I pray that God, who gives hope, will bless you with
complete happiness and peace because of your faith.
And may the power of the Holy Spirit fill you with hope.*

Rom. 15:13 CEV

In times of affliction we
commonly meet with the sweetest
experiences of the love of God.

John Bunyan

I wait quietly before God, for
my victory comes from Him.

Ps. 62:1 NLT

Therefore my heart is glad and my tongue
rejoices, my body also will rest secure.

Ps. 16:9 NIV

I lay down and slept; I woke again,
for the LORD sustained me.

Ps. 3:5 ESV

Abide with me, fast falls the eventide;
The darkness deepens; Lord, with me abide;
When other helpers fail and comforts flee,
Help of the helpless, oh, abide with me.

Henry Francis Lyte

The Lord your God will give you rest.

Deut. 12:10 NIV

God gives rest to His loved ones.

Ps. 127:2 NLT

*Those who walk uprightly enter
into peace; they find rest.*

Isa. 57:2 NIV

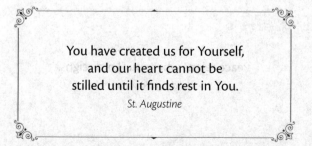

You have created us for Yourself,
and our heart cannot be
stilled until it finds rest in You.

St. Augustine

For thus said the Lord God, the Holy One of Israel,
"In returning and rest you shall be saved;
in quietness and in trust shall be your strength."
Isa. 30:15 ESV

So there is a special rest still waiting for the
people of God. For all who have entered into
God's rest have rested from their labors,
just as God did after creating the world.
Heb. 4:9-10 NLT

Oh, that I had the wings of a dove!
I would fly away and be at rest.
Ps. 55:6 NIV

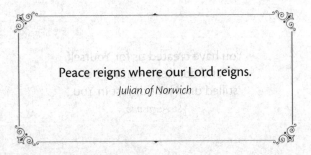

Peace reigns where our Lord reigns.
Julian of Norwich

*I pray that God the Father and Jesus Christ
His Son will be kind and merciful to us!
May they give us peace and truth and love.*
2 John 1:3 CEV

*Let the peace of Christ rule in your
hearts, to which indeed you were
called in one body. And be thankful.*
Col. 3:15 ESV

*He grants peace to your borders and
satisfies you with the finest of wheat.*
Ps. 147:14 NIV

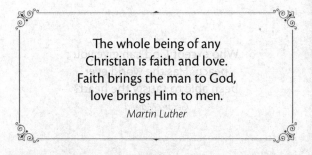

The whole being of any
Christian is faith and love.
Faith brings the man to God,
love brings Him to men.
Martin Luther

You will give us peace, LORD, because
everything we have done was by Your power.
Isa. 26:12 CEV

Therefore, since we have been made
right in God's sight by faith, we have
peace with God because of what
Jesus Christ our Lord has done for us.
Rom. 5:1 NLT

May mercy, peace, and
love be multiplied to you.
Jude 2 ESV

Who except God can give you
peace? Has the world ever
been able to satisfy the heart?
Gerard Majella

"No matter where you are, I, the LORD,
will heal you and give you peace."

Isa. 57:19 CEV

What you have learned and received and
heard and seen in me – practice these things,
and the God of peace will be with you.

Phil. 4:9 ESV

He was pierced for our transgressions,
He was crushed for our iniquities; the
punishment that brought us peace was on
Him, and by His wounds we are healed.

Isa. 53:5 NIV

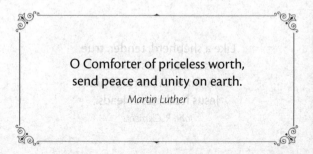

O Comforter of priceless worth,
send peace and unity on earth.

Martin Luther

"I Myself will tend My sheep and give them a place to lie down in peace," says the Sovereign LORD.
Ezek. 34:15 NLT

When the chief Shepherd appears, you will receive the unfading crown of glory.
1 Pet. 5:4 ESV

God's Spirit makes us peaceful.
Gal. 5:22 CEV

Like a shepherd, tender, true,
Jesus leads, Jesus leads,
Daily finds us pastures new,
Jesus leads, Jesus leads.

John R. Clements

"My presence will go with you,
and I will give you rest."
Exod. 33:14 ESV

The mind governed by the flesh is death, but the
mind governed by the Spirit is life and peace.
Rom. 8:6 NIV

Justice will produce lasting peace and
security. You, the LORD's people,
will live in peace, calm and secure.
Isa. 32:17-18 CEV

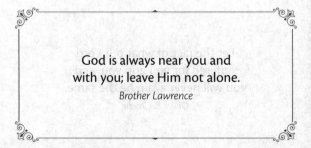

God is always near you and
with you; leave Him not alone.
Brother Lawrence

Since He Himself has gone through suffering and testing,
He is able to help us when we are being tested.

Heb. 2:18 NLT

For if, while we were God's enemies, we were
reconciled to Him through the death of His Son,
how much more, having been reconciled,
shall we be saved through His life!

Rom. 5:10 NIV

My friends, be glad, even if you have a lot of
trouble. You know that you learn to endure by
having your faith tested. But you must learn
to endure everything, so that you will be
completely mature and not lacking in anything.

James 1:2-4 CEV

Let the fact of what our Lord
suffered for you grip you, and
you will never again be the same.

Oliver B. Greene

They bowed down and worshiped the LORD
because they knew that He had seen their
suffering and was going to help them.
Exod. 4:31 CEV

You have faith in God, whose power
will protect you until the last day.
Then He will save you, just as
He has always planned to do.
1 Pet. 1: 5 CEV

He came and preached peace to you who
were far off and peace to those who were near.
Eph. 2:17 ESV

Ask the Savior to help you,
comfort, strengthen and keep
you; He is willing to aid you,
He will carry you through.

Horatio R. Palmer

I pray that God, who gives peace,
will make you completely holy.

1 Thess. 5:23 CEV

The LORD gives His people strength.
The LORD blesses them with peace.

Ps. 29:11 NLT

God gave us a spirit not of fear but of
power and love and self-control.

2 Tim. 1:7 ESV

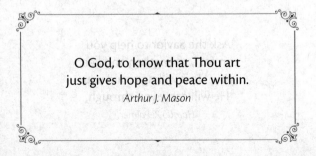

O God, to know that Thou art
just gives hope and peace within.

Arthur J. Mason

When you are suffering and in need,
He will come to your rescue.

Ps. 107:41 CEV

For the moment all discipline seems painful
rather than pleasant, but later it yields
the peaceful fruit of righteousness to
those who have been trained by it.

Heb. 12:11 ESV

We can rejoice, too, when we run into problems and trials,
for we know that they help us develop endurance.
And endurance develops strength of character, and
character strengthens our confident hope of salvation.

Rom. 5:3-4 NLT

Don't think so much about who is for or
against you, rather give all your care, that
God be with you in everything you do.

Thomas à Kempis

He took up our pain and bore our suffering.

Isa. 53:4 NIV

*God blesses those who patiently endure testing and
temptation. Afterward they will receive the crown of
life that God has promised to those who love Him.*

James 1:12 NLT

*We are afflicted in every way, but not crushed;
perplexed, but not driven to despair; persecuted,
but not forsaken; struck down, but not destroyed.*

2 Cor. 4:8-9 ESV

The bitter herbs of Gethsemane have
often taken away the bitters of your life;
the scourge of Gabbatha hath often scourged
away your cares, and the groans of Calvary
have put all other groans to flight.

Charles H. Spurgeon

He will wipe all tears from their eyes,
and there will be no more death,
suffering, crying, or pain.

Rev. 21:4 CEV

There will be no more night. They will not need
the light of a lamp or the light of the sun,
for the Lord God will give them light.
And they will reign for ever and ever.

Rev. 22:5 NIV

After my skin has been destroyed, yet in
my flesh I will see God; I myself will see Him
with my own eyes – I, and not another.
How my heart yearns within me.

Job 19:26-27 NIV

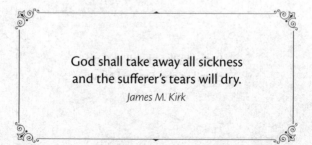

God shall take away all sickness
and the sufferer's tears will dry.

James M. Kirk

Jesus said, "Why do you ask Me about what is
good? Only God is good. If you want to have
eternal life, you must obey His commandments."

Matt. 19:17 CEV

Whoever sows to please their flesh,
from the flesh will reap destruction;
whoever sows to please the Spirit,
from the Spirit will reap eternal life.

Gal. 6:8 NIV

"I tell you the truth, anyone
who believes has eternal life."

John 6:47 NLT

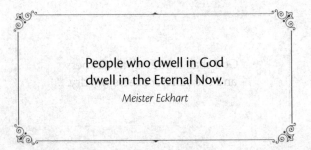

People who dwell in God
dwell in the Eternal Now.

Meister Eckhart

The Lord knows how to rescue godly people
from their trials, even while keeping the wicked
under punishment until the day of final judgment.

2 Pet. 2:9 NLT

I will listen to You, LORD God, because You promise
peace to those who are faithful and no longer foolish.

Ps. 85:8 CEV

"Peace I leave with you; My peace I give
to you. Not as the world gives do I
give to you. Let not your hearts be
troubled, neither let them be afraid."

John 14:27 ESV

When spiritual comfort is sent to you by God,
take it humbly and give thanks meekly for it.
But know for certain that it is the great
goodness of God that sends it to you.

Thomas à Kempis

"The righteous will go into eternal life."

Matt. 25:46 NLT

*"There are many rooms in My Father's house.
I wouldn't tell you this, unless it was true.
I am going there to prepare a place for each
of you. After I have done this, I will come back
and take you with Me. Then we will be together."*

John 14:2-3 CEV

*Your dead shall live; their bodies shall rise.
You who dwell in the dust, awake and sing
for joy! For your dew is a dew of light,
and the earth will give birth to the dead.*

Isa. 26:19 ESV

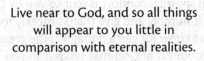

Live near to God, and so all things
will appear to you little in
comparison with eternal realities.

Robert Murray McCheyne

"Everyone who believes in Him will have eternal life."
John 3:15 NLT

All of you have faith in the Son of God,
and I have written to let you
know that you have eternal life.
1 John 5:13 CEV

It has now been revealed through the
appearing of our Savior, Christ Jesus, who
has destroyed death and has brought life
and immortality to light through the gospel.
2 Tim. 1:10 NIV

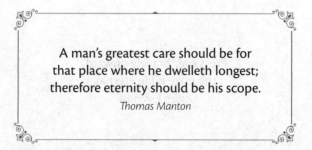

A man's greatest care should be for
that place where he dwelleth longest;
therefore eternity should be his scope.
Thomas Manton

"Those who have done good will
rise to experience eternal life."
John 5:29 NLT

You search the Scriptures because
you think they give you eternal life.
But the Scriptures point to Me!"
John 5:39 NIV

"If you love your life, you will lose it.
If you give it up in this world,
you will be given eternal life."
John 12:25 CEV

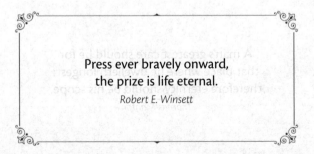

Press ever bravely onward,
the prize is life eternal.
Robert E. Winsett

*"My Father's will is that everyone
who looks to the Son and believes
in Him shall have eternal life."*
John 6:40 NIV

*This is what God has testified:
He has given us eternal life,
and this life is in His Son.*
1 John 5:11 NLT

*"I am the resurrection and the life.
Whoever believes in Me, though he die,
yet shall he live, and everyone who
lives and believes in Me shall never die."*
John 11:25-26 ESV

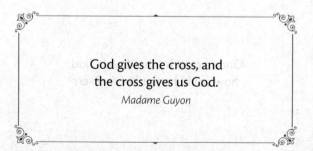

God gives the cross, and
the cross gives us God.

Madame Guyon

*"This is the way to have eternal life –
to know You, the only true God, and
Jesus Christ, the One You sent to earth."*
John 17:3 NLT

*"Whoever eats My flesh and drinks
My blood has eternal life, and I
will raise them up at the last day."*
John 6:54 NIV

*For the Lord Himself will descend from
heaven with a cry of command, with
the voice of an archangel, and with
the sound of the trumpet of God.
And the dead in Christ will rise first.*
1 Thess. 4:16 ESV

Once a man is united with God,
how could he not live forever?

C. S. Lewis

*The free gift of God is eternal
life in Christ Jesus our Lord.*
Rom. 6:23 ESV

This is what He promised us – eternal life.
1 John 2:25 NIV

*The Spirit of God, who raised Jesus from the dead,
lives in you. And just as God raised Christ Jesus
from the dead, He will give life to your mortal
bodies by this same Spirit living within you.*
Rom. 8:11 NLT

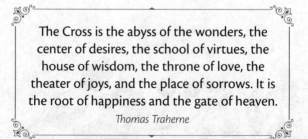

The Cross is the abyss of the wonders, the
center of desires, the school of virtues, the
house of wisdom, the throne of love, the
theater of joys, and the place of sorrows. It is
the root of happiness and the gate of heaven.

Thomas Traherne

April

God is merciful, just and fair.

How glorious is our God! He is
the Rock; His deeds are perfect.
Everything He does is just and fair.

Deut. 32:3-4 NLT

For the LORD loves justice;
He will not forsake His saints.
They are preserved forever.

Ps. 37:28 ESV

God is just: He will pay back
trouble to those who trouble you.

2 Thess. 1:6 NIV

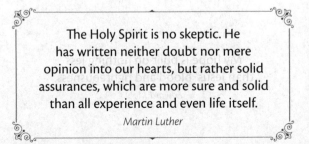

The Holy Spirit is no skeptic. He
has written neither doubt nor mere
opinion into our hearts, but rather solid
assurances, which are more sure and solid
than all experience and even life itself.

Martin Luther

The LORD your God's decisions are always fair.

Deut. 10:17 CEV

O LORD, You are righteous,
and Your regulations are fair.

Ps. 119:137 NLT

For God shows no partiality.

Rom. 2:11 ESV

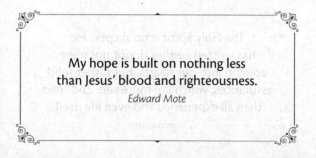

My hope is built on nothing less
than Jesus' blood and righteousness.

Edward Mote

Although God is mighty, He cares about
everyone and makes fair decisions.
Job 36:5 CEV

The LORD is good to everyone.
He showers compassion on all His creation.
Ps. 145:9 NLT

Just as parents are kind to their children,
the LORD is kind to all who worship Him.
Ps. 103:13 CEV

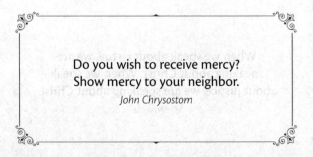

Do you wish to receive mercy?
Show mercy to your neighbor.
John Chrysostom

*The laws of the L*ORD *are true; each one is fair.*

Ps. 19:9 NLT

Your righteousness is righteous forever,
and Your law is true.

Ps. 119:142 ESV

Truly I understand that God shows no partiality.

Acts 10:34 ESV

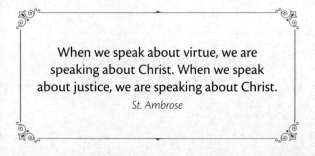

When we speak about virtue, we are
speaking about Christ. When we speak
about justice, we are speaking about Christ.

St. Ambrose

"I am a merciful God."
Exod. 22:27 CEV

*God presented Christ as a sacrifice of atonement ...
He did it to demonstrate His righteousness at
the present time, so as to be just and the One
who justifies those who have faith in Jesus.*
Rom. 3:25-26 NIV

*The LORD is righteous in everything
He does; He is filled with kindness.*
Ps. 145:17 NLT

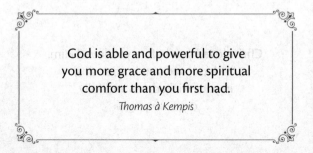

**God is able and powerful to give
you more grace and more spiritual
comfort than you first had.**
Thomas à Kempis

*The Lord your God is a merciful
God. He will not leave you.*

Deut. 4:31 ESV

*God our Savior showed us how good and kind He is.
He saved us because of His mercy and not
because of any good things that we have done.*

Titus 3:4-5 CEV

*He shows mercy from generation
to generation to all who fear Him.*

Luke 1:50 NLT

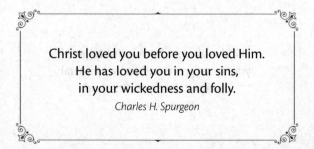

Christ loved you before you loved Him.
He has loved you in your sins,
in your wickedness and folly.

Charles H. Spurgeon

The LORD your God is gracious and merciful
and will not turn away His face from you.
2 Chron. 30:9 ESV

Because of the LORD's great love we are not consumed,
for His compassions never fail. They are new
every morning; great is Your faithfulness.
Lam. 3:22-23 NIV

The grace of God has been revealed,
bringing salvation to all people.
Titus 2:11 NLT

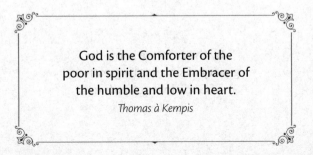

God is the Comforter of the
poor in spirit and the Embracer of
the humble and low in heart.

Thomas à Kempis

*The Lord God is famous for His wonderful
deeds, and He is kind and merciful.*
Ps. 111:4 CEV

*Your righteousness, O God, reaches the
high heavens. You who have done
great things, O God, who is like You?*
Ps. 71:19 ESV

*We cannot imagine the power of the
Almighty; but even though He is just
and righteous, He does not destroy us.*
Job 37:23 NLT

By the cross we know the
gravity of sin and the greatness
of God's love towards us.

John Chrysostom

How kind the LORD is! How good He is!
So merciful, this God of ours!
Ps. 116:5 NLT

"I will scatter the seeds and show mercy."
Hos. 2:23 CEV

"Blessed are the merciful,
for they shall receive mercy."
Matt. 5:7 ESV

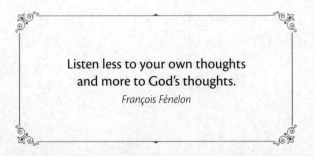

Listen less to your own thoughts
and more to God's thoughts.
François Fénelon

The LORD your God is merciful and compassionate,
slow to get angry and filled with unfailing love.
Joel 2:13 NLT

Everything the LORD does is glorious and majestic,
and His power to bring justice will never end.
Ps. 111:3 CEV

Blessed are they who observe justice,
who do righteousness at all times!
Ps. 106:3 ESV

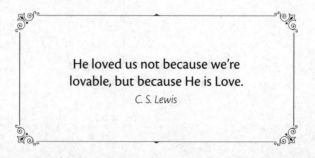

He loved us not because we're
lovable, but because He is Love.

C. S. Lewis

*Let us fall into the hands of the
LORD, for His mercy is great.*
2 Sam. 24:14 NLT

*Because of the tender mercy of our God ... the
rising sun will come to us from heaven to shine
on those living in darkness and in the shadow
of death, to guide our feet into the path of peace.*
Luke 1:78-79 NIV

*God is always fair. He will remember how you
helped His people in the past and how you are
still helping them. You belong to God, and He
won't forget the love you have shown His people.*
Heb. 6:10 CEV

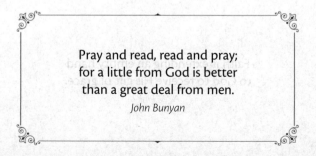

Pray and read, read and pray;
for a little from God is better
than a great deal from men.

John Bunyan

*Surely Your goodness and love will follow
me all the days of my life, and I will
dwell in the house of the LORD forever.*

Ps. 23:6 NIV

*"Be merciful, even as your Father is merciful.
Judge not, and you will not be judged;
condemn not, and you will not be condemned;
forgive, and you will be forgiven."*

Luke 6:36-37 ESV

*They will neither hunger nor thirst.
The searing sun will not reach them anymore.
For the LORD in His mercy will lead them;
He will lead them beside cool waters.*

Isa. 49:10 NLT

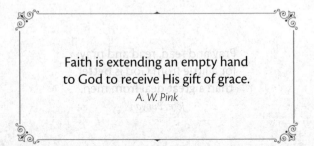

Faith is extending an empty hand
to God to receive His gift of grace.

A. W. Pink

Praise be to the Lᴏʀᴅ, for He
has heard my cry for mercy.
Ps. 28:6 ɴɪᴠ

"Plow your fields, scatter seeds of
justice, and harvest faithfulness.
Worship Me, the Lᴏʀᴅ, and I will send
My saving power down like rain."
Hos. 10:12 ᴄᴇᴠ

"I will make all My goodness pass before you and
will proclaim before you My name 'The Lᴏʀᴅ.'
And I will be gracious to whom I will be gracious,
and will show mercy on whom I will show mercy."
Exod. 33:19 ᴇsᴠ

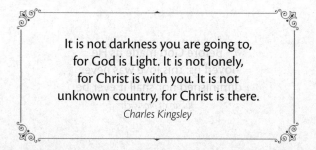

It is not darkness you are going to,
for God is Light. It is not lonely,
for Christ is with you. It is not
unknown country, for Christ is there.
Charles Kingsley

*In panic I cried out, "I am cut off from
the Lord!" But You heard my cry for
mercy and answered my call for help.*
Ps. 31:22 NLT

*Remember Your mercy, O Lord,
and Your steadfast love, for
they have been from of old.*
Ps. 25:6 ESV

*I am Your servant, so please have
mercy on me and answer the
prayer that I make day and night.*
Neh. 1:5-6 CEV

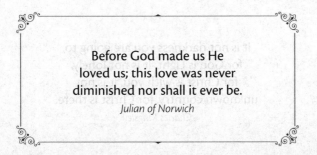

**Before God made us He
loved us; this love was never
diminished nor shall it ever be.**
Julian of Norwich

The Lord is full of compassion and mercy.
James 5:11 NIV

The LORD is compassionate and merciful,
slow to get angry and filled with unfailing love.
Ps. 103:8 NLT

You, O Lord, are a God merciful and gracious.
Ps. 86:15 ESV

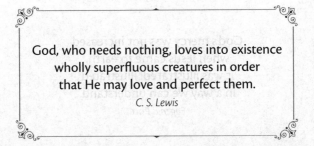

God, who needs nothing, loves into existence
wholly superfluous creatures in order
that He may love and perfect them.

C. S. Lewis

*Let every true worshiper of the
LORD shout, "God is always merciful!"*
Ps. 118:4 CEV

*Wealth and riches are in His house,
and His righteousness endures forever.*
Ps. 112:3 ESV

*The law of the LORD is perfect,
refreshing the soul.*
Ps. 19:7 NIV

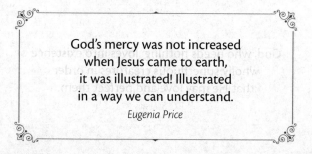

God's mercy was not increased
when Jesus came to earth,
it was illustrated! Illustrated
in a way we can understand.

Eugenia Price

The Lord our God is merciful and forgiving.
Dan. 9:9 NLT

*A person may think their own ways are
right, but the LORD weighs the heart.*
Prov. 21:2 NIV

*"Keep justice, and do righteousness,
for soon My salvation will come,
and My righteousness be revealed."*
Isa. 56:1 ESV

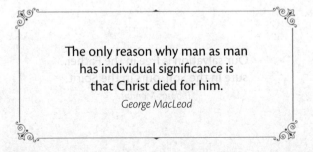

The only reason why man as man
has individual significance is
that Christ died for him.
George MacLeod

God was merciful! We were dead because of our sins,
but God loved us so much that He made us alive with
Christ, and God's wonderful kindness is what saves you.

Eph. 2:4 CEV

Whoever pursues righteousness
and kindness will find life,
righteousness, and honor.

Prov. 21:21 ESV

By steadfast love and faithfulness iniquity is atoned for,
and by the fear of the LORD one turns away from evil.

Prov. 16:6 ESV

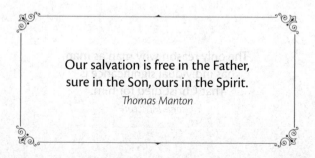

Our salvation is free in the Father,
sure in the Son, ours in the Spirit.

Thomas Manton

Even in judgment, God is merciful!
James 2:13 CEV

When a king sits in judgment,
he weighs all the evidence,
distinguishing the bad from the good.
Prov. 20:8 NLT

Let the wicked forsake their ways
and the unrighteous their thoughts.
Let them turn to the LORD, and
He will have mercy on them, and
to our God, for He will freely pardon.
Isa. 55:7 NIV

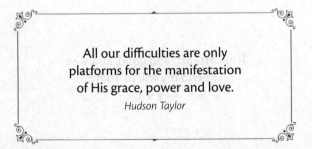

All our difficulties are only
platforms for the manifestation
of His grace, power and love.
Hudson Taylor

God cannot be seen – but His power
is great, and He is always fair.
Job 37:23 CEV

Clouds and thick darkness are all
around Him; righteousness and justice
are the foundation of His throne.
Ps. 97:2 ESV

Masters, be just and fair to your slaves. Remember
that you also have a Master – in heaven.
Col. 4:1 NLT

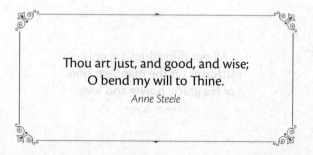

Thou art just, and good, and wise;
O bend my will to Thine.
Anne Steele

*The LORD does right and is always fair. With the
dawn of each day, God brings about justice.*
Zeph. 3:5 CEV

"The Lord will judge His people."
Heb. 10:30 NIV

*The LORD loves justice, and
He will never abandon the godly.
He will keep them safe forever.*
Ps. 37:28 NLT

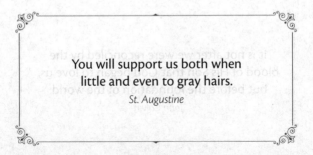

You will support us both when
little and even to gray hairs.
St. Augustine

God is always fair.
Heb. 6:10 CEV

"He is kind to the ungrateful and wicked."
Luke 6:35 NIV

When justice is done, it is a joy to the righteous.
Prov. 21:15 ESV

It is not after we were reconciled by the
blood of His Son that God began to love us,
but before the foundation of the world.
John Calvin

This faith was given to you
because of the justice and fairness
of Jesus Christ, our God and Savior.
2 Pet. 1:1 NLT

He is the LORD our God;
His judgments are in all the earth.
1 Chron. 16:14 NIV

Blessed are they who observe justice,
who do righteousness at all times!
Ps. 106:3 ESV

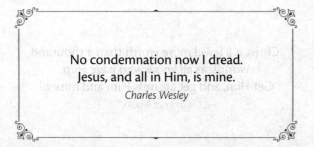

No condemnation now I dread.
Jesus, and all in Him, is mine.
Charles Wesley

*Lord God All-Powerful, You have done great
and marvelous things. You are the ruler of
all nations, and You do what is right and fair.*
Rev. 15:3 CEV

He loves whatever is just and good.
Ps. 33:5 NLT

*For the LORD is righteous,
He loves justice.*
Ps. 11:7 NIV

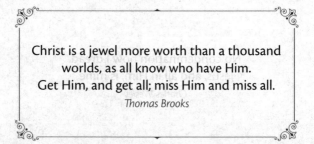

Christ is a jewel more worth than a thousand
worlds, as all know who have Him.
Get Him, and get all; miss Him and miss all.

Thomas Brooks

The LORD has heard my cry for mercy;
the LORD accepts my prayer.

Ps. 6:9 NIV

Whenever we are in need, we should come
bravely before the throne of our merciful God.
There we will be treated with undeserved kindness,
and we will find help.

Heb. 4:16 CEV

The love of the LORD remains forever with
those who fear Him. His salvation
extends to the children's children.

Ps. 103:17 NLT

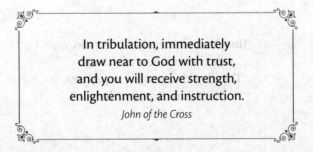

In tribulation, immediately
draw near to God with trust,
and you will receive strength,
enlightenment, and instruction.

John of the Cross

Great is Your mercy, O LORD;
give me life according to Your rules.

Ps. 119:156 ESV

"I am the LORD God. I am merciful
and very patient with My people.
I show great love, and I can be trusted."

Exod. 34:6 CEV

Let us then approach God's throne of grace
with confidence, so that we may receive mercy
and find grace to help us in our time of need.

Heb. 4:16 NIV

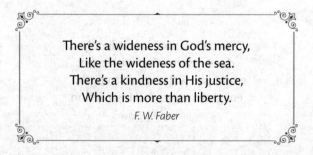

There's a wideness in God's mercy,
Like the wideness of the sea.
There's a kindness in His justice,
Which is more than liberty.

F. W. Faber

Therefore the LORD waits to be gracious to you,
and therefore He exalts Himself to show mercy
to you. For the LORD is a God of justice;
blessed are all those who wait for Him.
Isa. 30:18 ESV

The grace of the Lord Jesus Christ be with your spirit.
Phil. 4:23 ESV

God is able to make all grace abound to you, so
that having all sufficiency in all things at all
times, you may abound in every good work.
2 Cor. 9:8 ESV

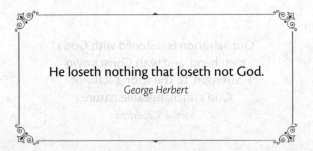

He loseth nothing that loseth not God.
George Herbert

All praise to God, the Father of our Lord Jesus Christ.
It is by His great mercy that we have been born again.
1 Pet. 1:3 NLT

LORD God, You are merciful and forgiving,
even though we have rebelled against You.
Dan. 9:9 CEV

You will surely forget your trouble,
recalling it only as waters gone by.
Job 11:16 NIV

Our salvation is fastened with God's
own hand, and with Christ's own
strength, to the strong stake of
God's unchangeable nature.
Samuel Rutherford

Await the mercy of our Lord Jesus Christ,
who will bring you eternal life.
Jude 1:21 NLT

But you must return to your God;
maintain love and justice,
and wait for your God always.
Hos. 12:6 NIV

The LORD is merciful and gracious, slow to
anger and abounding in steadfast love.
Ps. 103:8 ESV

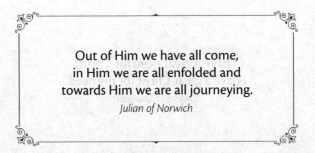

Out of Him we have all come,
in Him we are all enfolded and
towards Him we are all journeying.
Julian of Norwich

Whenever I complain to You, Lord, You are always fair.
Jer. 12:1 CEV

He is the Rock; His deeds are perfect.
Everything He does is just and fair.
He is a faithful God who does no wrong;
how just and upright He is.
Deut. 32:4 NLT

If we confess our sins, He is faithful
and just and will forgive us our sins
and purify us from all unrighteousness.
1 John 1:9 NIV

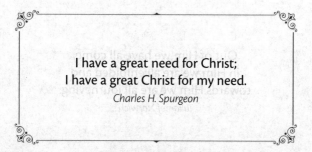

I have a great need for Christ;
I have a great Christ for my need.
Charles H. Spurgeon

May

God gives you a reason to rejoice,
be happy and have hope.

*May the God of hope fill you with all joy and
peace as you trust in Him, so that you may
overflow with hope by the power of the Holy Spirit.*
Rom. 15:13 NIV

*We look forward with hope to that wonderful
day when the glory of our great God
and Savior, Jesus Christ, will be revealed.*
Titus 2:13 NLT

*This hope is what saves us. But if
we already have what we hope for,
there is no need to keep on hoping.
However, we hope for something we have
not yet seen, and we patiently wait for it.*
Rom. 8:24-25 CEV

The word "hope" I take for faith;
and indeed hope is nothing
else but the constancy of faith.
John Calvin

"I know the plans I have for you,"
says the Lord. "They are plans for
good and not for disaster, to give
you a future and a hope."
Jer. 29:11 NLT

I am waiting for You, O Lord.
You must answer for me, O Lord my God.
Ps. 38:15 NLT

Blessed is the one who trusts in the Lord,
whose confidence is in Him.
Jer. 17:7 NIV

The future is as bright as
the promises of God.
Adoniram Judson

May integrity and honesty protect me,
for I put my hope in You.
Ps. 25:21 NLT

I have the same hope in God as these men
themselves have, that there will be a resurrection
of both the righteous and the wicked.
Acts 24:15 NIV

If in Christ we have hope in this life only,
we are of all people most to be pitied.
1 Cor. 15:19 ESV

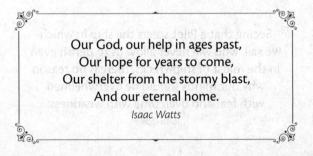

Our God, our help in ages past,
Our hope for years to come,
Our shelter from the stormy blast,
And our eternal home.

Isaac Watts

Be strong and take heart,
all you who hope in the LORD.
Ps. 31:24 NIV

O Lord, You alone are my hope.
I've trusted You, O LORD, from childhood.
Ps. 71:5 NLT

Everyone who thus hopes in Him
purifies himself as He is pure.
1 John 3:3 ESV

Seeing that a Pilot steers the ship in which
we sail, who will never allow us to perish even
in the midst of shipwrecks, there is no reason
why our minds should be overwhelmed
with fear and overcome with weariness.

John Calvin

The LORD is good to those whose hope is in Him.
Lam. 3:25 NIV

*We have this as a sure and steadfast
anchor of the soul, a hope that enters
into the inner place behind the curtain.*
Heb. 6:19 ESV

*The hopes of the godly result in happiness, but
the expectations of the wicked come to nothing.*
Prov. 10:28 NLT

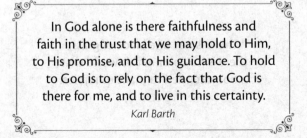

In God alone is there faithfulness and
faith in the trust that we may hold to Him,
to His promise, and to His guidance. To hold
to God is to rely on the fact that God is
there for me, and to live in this certainty.

Karl Barth

Let Your unfailing love surround us,
LORD, for our hope is in You alone.

Ps. 33:22 NLT

You are my refuge and my shield;
I have put my hope in Your word.

Ps. 119:114 NIV

You are my only hope for being saved,
LORD, and I do all You command.

Ps. 119:166 CEV

There is not one blade of grass,
there is no color in this world that
is not intended to make us rejoice.

John Calvin

The Lord will make you successful in everything
you do. You will be completely happy.
Deut. 16:13-15 cev

May you be filled with joy, always thanking the Father.
He has enabled you to share in the inheritance that
belongs to His people, who live in the light.
Col. 1:11-12 nlt

Blessed is the one whom God reproves;
therefore despise not the discipline of the Almighty.
Job 5:17 esv

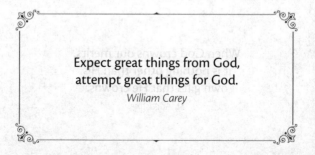

Expect great things from God,
attempt great things for God.
William Carey

*To the person who pleases Him, God gives
wisdom, knowledge and happiness.*
Eccles. 2:26 NIV

*May the glory of the LORD continue forever!
The LORD takes pleasure in all He has made!*
Ps. 104:31 NLT

*Great are the works of the LORD,
studied by all who delight in them.*
Ps. 111:2 ESV

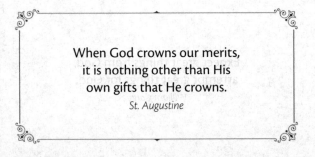

When God crowns our merits,
it is nothing other than His
own gifts that He crowns.

St. Augustine

You make me strong and happy, LORD.
1 Sam. 2:1 CEV

So rejoice in the LORD and be glad,
all you who obey Him!
Ps. 32:11 NLT

Do not be grieved, for the joy
of the LORD is your strength.
Neh. 8:10 ESV

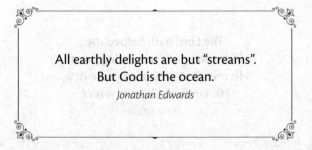

All earthly delights are but "streams".
But God is the ocean.
Jonathan Edwards

LORD God, You have shown great
kindness to us. You made us truly happy.

Ezra 9:8 CEV

There you and your families will feast in the
presence of the LORD your God, and you
will rejoice in all you have accomplished
because the LORD your God has blessed you.

Deut. 12:7 NLT

For great is His steadfast love
toward us, and the faithfulness of the
LORD endures forever. Praise the LORD!

Ps. 117:2 ESV

The Lord hath helped me
hitherto by His surpassing favor;
His mercies every morn were new,
His kindness did not waver.

Ämilie Juliane

You thrill me, LORD, with all You have done for me!
I sing for joy because of what You have done.
Ps. 92:4 NLT

Because Your love is better than life,
my lips will glorify You.
Ps. 63:3 NIV

When he came and saw the grace of God,
he was glad, and he exhorted them all to remain
faithful to the Lord with steadfast purpose.
Acts 11:23 ESV

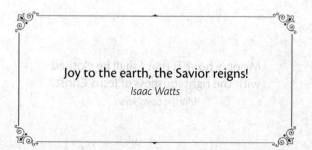

Joy to the earth, the Savior reigns!
Isaac Watts

I will greatly rejoice in the LORD; my soul shall exult in my God, for He has clothed me with the garments of salvation; He has covered me with the robe of righteousness.

Isa. 61:10 ESV

*As for me, I will always have hope;
I will praise You more and more.*

Ps. 71:14 NIV

*Let all who run to You for protection always
sing joyful songs. Provide shelter for those
who truly love You and let them rejoice.*

Ps. 5:11 CEV

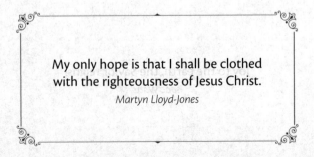

My only hope is that I shall be clothed
with the righteousness of Jesus Christ.

Martyn Lloyd-Jones

"You have not asked for anything in this way before,
but now you must ask in My name. Then it will be
given to you, so that you will be completely happy."
John 16:24 CEV

I will rejoice in the LORD! I will be
joyful in the God of my salvation!
Hab. 3:18 NLT

"Do not rejoice in this, that the spirits are subject to you,
but rejoice that your names are written in heaven."
Luke 10:20 ESV

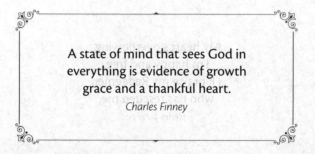

A state of mind that sees God in
everything is evidence of growth
grace and a thankful heart.
Charles Finney

I will rejoice because the LORD has rescued me.

Ps. 13:5 NLT

Why am I discouraged? Why am I restless?
I trust You! And I will praise You again because
You help me, and You are my God.

Ps. 42:11 CEV

Rejoice ... your King is coming to you.

Zech. 9:9 ESV

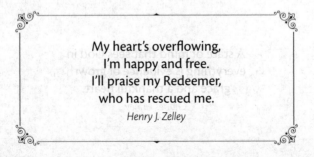

My heart's overflowing,
I'm happy and free.
I'll praise my Redeemer,
who has rescued me.

Henry J. Zelley

Glory in His holy name; let the hearts
of those who seek the LORD rejoice.
1 Chron. 16:10 NIV

May all who seek You rejoice and be glad in You;
may those who love Your salvation say continually,
"Great is the LORD!"
Ps. 40:16 ESV

Yes, the LORD has done amazing
things for us! What joy!
Ps. 126:3 NLT

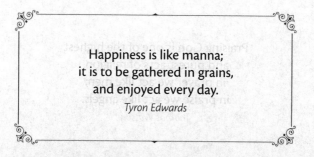

Happiness is like manna;
it is to be gathered in grains,
and enjoyed every day.
Tyron Edwards

The LORD is King! Let the earth rejoice!
Let the farthest coastlands be glad.

Ps. 97:1 NLT

Rejoice always!
1 Thess. 5:16 ESV

Shout for joy to the LORD,
all the earth.
Ps. 100:1 NIV

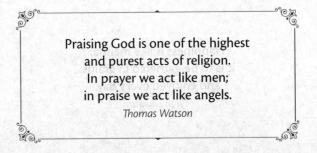

Praising God is one of the highest
and purest acts of religion.
In prayer we act like men;
in praise we act like angels.

Thomas Watson

This is the day that the LORD has made;
let us rejoice and be glad in it.
Ps. 118:24 ESV

Rejoice in the Lord always.
I will say it again: Rejoice!
Phil. 4:4 NIV

True godliness with contentment
is itself great wealth.
1 Tim. 6:6 NLT

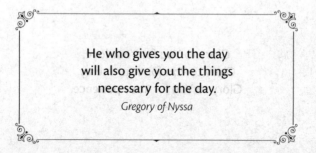

He who gives you the day
will also give you the things
necessary for the day.
Gregory of Nyssa

Let the heavens be glad, and let
the earth rejoice, and let them say
among the nations, "The LORD reigns!"

1 Chron. 16:31 ESV

Rejoice before the LORD your God.

Deut. 16:11 NIV

Through Christ you have come to trust in God.
And you have placed your faith and
hope in God because He raised Christ
from the dead and gave Him great glory.

1 Pet. 1:21 NLT

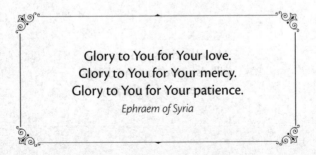

Glory to You for Your love.
Glory to You for Your mercy.
Glory to You for Your patience.

Ephraem of Syria

The LORD is good to everyone. He showers
compassion on all His creation.

Ps. 145:9 NLT

My prayer is that light will flood your hearts
and that you will understand the hope
that was given to you when God chose you.
Then you will discover the glorious blessings
that will be yours together with all of God's people.

Eph. 1:18 CEV

Give thanks to the LORD, for He is good,
for His steadfast love endures forever.

Ps. 136:1 ESV

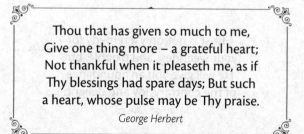

Thou that has given so much to me,
Give one thing more – a grateful heart;
Not thankful when it pleaseth me, as if
Thy blessings had spare days; But such
a heart, whose pulse may be Thy praise.

George Herbert

*The Lord renews our hopes
and heals our bodies.*

Ps. 147:3 CEV

*Prepare your minds for action and exercise self-control.
Put all your hope in the gracious salvation that will
come to you when Jesus Christ is revealed to the world.*

1 Pet. 1:13 NLT

*All of you are part of the same body. There is only
one Spirit of God, just as you were given one
hope when you were chosen to be God's people*

Eph. 4:4 CEV

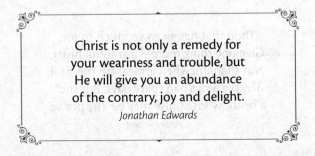

Christ is not only a remedy for
your weariness and trouble, but
He will give you an abundance
of the contrary, joy and delight.

Jonathan Edwards

"*Know that I am the* LORD; *those who hope in Me will not be disappointed.*"
Isa. 49:23 NIV

Honor Christ and let Him be the Lord of your life. Always be ready to give an answer when someone asks you about your hope.
1 Pet. 3:15 CEV

Our great desire is that you will keep on loving others as long as life lasts, in order to make certain that what you hope for will come true.
Heb. 6:11 NLT

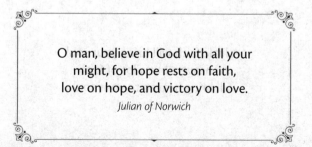

O man, believe in God with all your might, for hope rests on faith, love on hope, and victory on love.
Julian of Norwich

*The Scriptures say that no one who
has faith will be disappointed.*

Rom. 10:11 CEV

*My soul longs for Your
salvation; I hope in Your word.*

Ps. 119:81 ESV

*Remember Your promise
to me; it is my only hope.*

Ps. 119:49 NLT

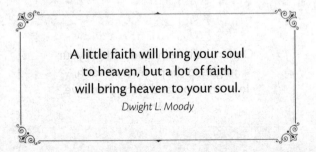

A little faith will bring your soul
to heaven, but a lot of faith
will bring heaven to your soul.

Dwight L. Moody

Hope will not lead to disappointment.
For we know how dearly God loves us.
Rom. 5:5 NLT

For through the Spirit we eagerly await by
faith the righteousness for which we hope.
Gal. 5:5 NIV

What you hope for is kept safe for you in heaven.
You first heard about this hope when you believed
the true message, which is the good news.
Col. 1:5 CEV

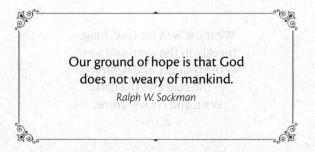

Our ground of hope is that God
does not weary of mankind.
Ralph W. Sockman

*God will give eternal life to everyone who has
patiently done what is good in the hope of
receiving glory, honor, and life that lasts forever.*

Rom. 2:7 CEV

*Having been justified by His grace, we might
become heirs having the hope of eternal life.*

Titus 3:7 NIV

*Those who listen to instruction will prosper;
those who trust the LORD will be joyful.*

Prov. 16:20 NLT

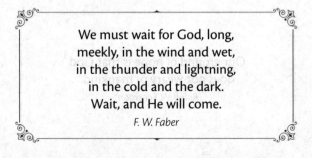

We must wait for God, long,
meekly, in the wind and wet,
in the thunder and lightning,
in the cold and the dark.
Wait, and He will come.

F. W. Faber

*God has accepted us because of Jesus Christ our
Lord. This means that we will have eternal life.*

Rom. 5:21 CEV

*Praise be to the God and Father of our Lord Jesus Christ!
In His great mercy He has given us new birth into a living
hope through the resurrection of Jesus Christ from the
dead.*

1 Pet. 1:3 NIV

*You lived in this world without God and without hope.
But now you have been united with Christ Jesus.
Once you were far away from God, but now you have
been brought near to Him through the blood of Christ.*

Eph. 2:12-13 NLT

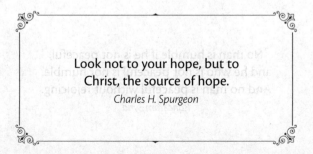

Look not to your hope, but to
Christ, the source of hope.

Charles H. Spurgeon

The humble will see their God at work and be glad.
Let all who seek God's help be encouraged.

Ps. 69:32 NLT

God is our refuge and strength,
a very present help in trouble.

Ps. 46:1 ESV

Humility is the fear of the LORD;
its wages are riches and honor and life.

Prov. 22:4 NIV

No man is humble if he is not peaceful,
and he who is not peaceful is not humble.
And no man is peaceful without rejoicing.

Isaac from Syria

No one who trusts in You will ever be disgraced.
Ps. 25:3 NLT

Since we have such a hope, we are very bold.
2 Cor. 3:12 ESV

*Through Him you believe in God, who raised
Him from the dead and glorified Him,
and so your faith and hope are in God.*
1 Pet. 1:21 NIV

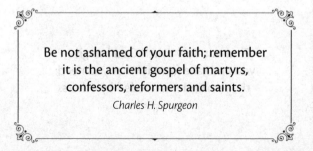

Be not ashamed of your faith; remember
it is the ancient gospel of martyrs,
confessors, reformers and saints.

Charles H. Spurgeon

Delight yourself in the LORD, and He will
give you the desires of your heart.
Ps. 37:4 ESV

I know the LORD is always with me. I will not be
shaken, for He is right beside me. No wonder my
heart is glad, and I rejoice. My body rests in safety.
Ps. 16:8-9 NLT

A happy heart makes the face cheerful.
Prov. 15:13 NIV

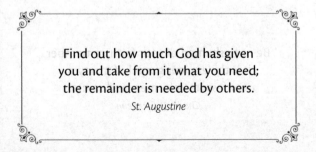

Find out how much God has given
you and take from it what you need;
the remainder is needed by others.

St. Augustine

*I consider that the sufferings of this
present time are not worth comparing
with the glory that is to be revealed to us.*
Rom. 8:18 ESV

*For just as we share abundantly in the sufferings of
Christ, so also our comfort abounds through Christ.*
2 Cor. 1:5 NIV

*We can rejoice, too, when we run into problems and trials,
for we know that they help us develop endurance.*
Rom. 5:3 NLT

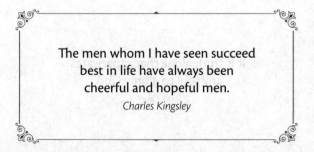

The men whom I have seen succeed
best in life have always been
cheerful and hopeful men.
Charles Kingsley

*Yes, what joy for those whose record the LORD has cleared
of guilt, whose lives are lived in complete honesty!*

Ps. 32:2 NLT

*You have shown me the path to life,
and You make me glad by being near to me.
Sitting at Your right side, I will always be joyful.*

Ps. 16:11 CEV

*With joy you will draw water
from the wells of salvation.*

Isa. 12:3 NIV

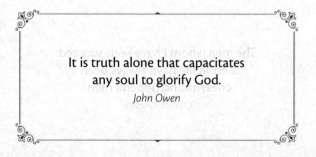

It is truth alone that capacitates
any soul to glorify God.
John Owen

Let the message about Christ, in all its richness,
fill your lives. Teach and counsel each
other with all the wisdom He gives.
Col. 3:16 NLT

For everything that was written in the past
was written to teach us, so that through the
endurance taught in the Scriptures and the
encouragement they provide we might have hope.
Rom. 15:4 NIV

Without guidance from God law and order disappear,
but God blesses everyone who obeys His Law.
Prov. 29:18 CEV

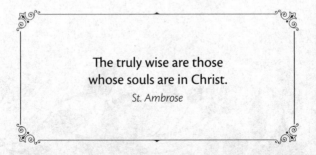

The truly wise are those
whose souls are in Christ.

St. Ambrose

June

God has a plan for your future,
and will grant you
wisdom for the journey.

I am trusting You, O Lord, saying, "You are my God!" My future is in Your hands.
Ps. 31:14-15 NLT

Give me wisdom and good sense. I trust Your commands.
Ps. 119:66 CEV

Those who listen to instruction will prosper; those who trust the Lord will be joyful.
Prov. 16:20 NLT

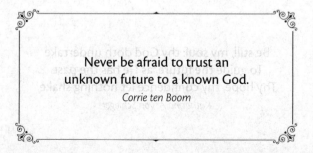

Never be afraid to trust an unknown future to a known God.
Corrie ten Boom

Always honor the LORD. Then you
will truly have hope for the future.
Prov. 23:17-18 CEV

The world is passing away along with its desires,
but whoever does the will of God abides forever.
1 John 2:17 ESV

My child, pay attention to what I say. Listen
carefully to my words. Don't lose sight of them.
Let them penetrate deep into your heart,
for they bring life to those who find them.
Prov. 4:20-22 NLT

Be still, my soul: thy God doth undertake
To guide the future, as He has the past.
Thy hope, thy confidence let nothing shake.

Katharina A. von Schlegel

"I am God, and there is none like Me. Only I
can tell you the future before it even happens."
Isa. 46:9-10 NLT

"Before I formed you in the womb I knew you,
before you were born I set you apart;
I appointed you as a prophet to the nations."
Jer. 1:5 NIV

Go in peace. The journey on which
you go is under the eye of the LORD.
Judg. 18:6 ESV

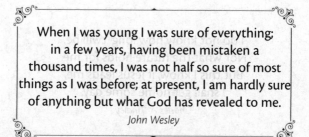

When I was young I was sure of everything;
in a few years, having been mistaken a
thousand times, I was not half so sure of most
things as I was before; at present, I am hardly sure
of anything but what God has revealed to me.

John Wesley

"There is hope for your future," declares the LORD.

Jer. 31:17 ESV

The LORD directs the steps of the godly.
He delights in every detail of their lives.

Ps. 37:23 NLT

He will teach us His ways, so
that we may walk in His paths.

Isa. 2:3 NIV

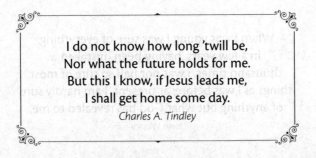

I do not know how long 'twill be,
Nor what the future holds for me.
But this I know, if Jesus leads me,
I shall get home some day.

Charles A. Tindley

"You can trust what I say about the future."
Hab. 2:3 CEV

My child listen to me and do as I say,
and you will have a long, good life.
Prov. 4:10 NLT

Now the LORD said to Abram, "Go from your
country and your kindred and your father's
house to the land that I will show you. And I will
make of you a great nation, and I will bless you and
make your name great, so that you will be a blessing."
Gen. 12:1-2 ESV

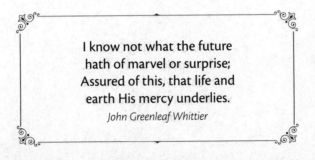

I know not what the future
hath of marvel or surprise;
Assured of this, that life and
earth His mercy underlies.
John Greenleaf Whittier

Let us hold tightly without wavering to the hope we
affirm, for God can be trusted to keep His promise.

Heb. 10:23 NLT

Do not be conformed to this world, but be
transformed by the renewal of your mind,
that by testing you may discern what is the will
of God, what is good and acceptable and perfect.

Rom. 12:2 ESV

"Come and set up Your kingdom, so
that everyone on earth will obey You,
as You are obeyed in heaven."

Matt. 6:10 CEV

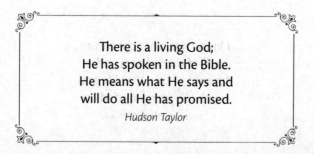

There is a living God;
He has spoken in the Bible.
He means what He says and
will do all He has promised.

Hudson Taylor

You, LORD God, have done many wonderful things,
and You have planned marvelous things for us.
Ps. 40:5 CEV

"To all who are victorious, who obey Me to the very end,
to them I will give authority over all the nations."
Rev. 2:26 NLT

"He will set you in praise and in fame
and in honor high above all nations that
He has made, and that you shall be a people
holy to the LORD your God, as He promised."
Deut. 26:19 ESV

He who leans only upon Christ,
lives the highest, choicest,
safest, and sweetest life.
Thomas Brooks

You, LORD, are my God! I will praise You
for doing the wonderful things You had
planned and promised since ancient times.

Isa. 25:1 CEV

Be thankful in all circumstances,
for this is God's will for you
who belong to Christ Jesus.

1 Thess. 5:18 NLT

Giving thanks always and for
everything to God the Father in
the name of our Lord Jesus Christ.

Eph. 5:20 ESV

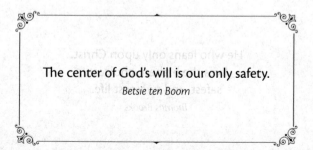

The center of God's will is our only safety.

Betsie ten Boom

In their hearts humans plan their course,
but the LORD establishes their steps.
Prov. 16:9 NIV

Let every person be subject to the governing
authorities. For there is no authority except from God,
and those that exist have been instituted by God.
Rom. 13:1 ESV

"I am the bread that gives life! No one who
comes to Me will ever be hungry. No one
who has faith in Me will ever be thirsty."
John 6:35 CEV

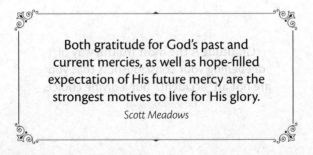

Both gratitude for God's past and
current mercies, as well as hope-filled
expectation of His future mercy are the
strongest motives to live for His glory.
Scott Meadows

I know, Lord, that our lives are not our own.
We are not able to plan our own course.
Jer. 10:23 NLT

The lot is cast into the lap, but its
every decision is from the Lord.
Prov. 16:33 NIV

This is the Lord's doing ... This is
the day that the Lord has made.
Ps. 118:23-24 ESV

Gratitude is the most fruitful way of
deepening your consciousness that you
are not an "accident," but a divine choice.
Henri Nouwen

*We are God's masterpiece. He has created
us anew in Christ Jesus, so we can do the
good things He planned for us long ago.*

Eph. 2:10 NLT

*Everything in the Scriptures is God's Word.
All of it is useful for teaching and helping
people and for correcting them and showing
them how to live. The Scriptures train
God's servants to do all kinds of good deeds.*

2 Tim. 3:16-18 CEV

*"In the same way, let your light shine before others,
so that they may see your good works and
give glory to your Father who is in heaven."*

Matt. 5:16 ESV

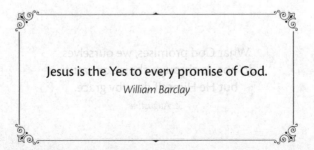

Jesus is the Yes to every promise of God.
William Barclay

The LORD's plans stand firm forever;
His intentions can never be shaken.

Ps. 33:11 NLT

"So that you may be sons of your Father who is in heaven.
For He makes His sun rise on the evil and on the good,
and sends rain on the just and on the unjust."

Matt. 5:45 ESV

Christ has also introduced us to God's undeserved
kindness on which we take our stand. So we are happy,
as we look forward to sharing in the glory of God.

Rom. 5:2 CEV

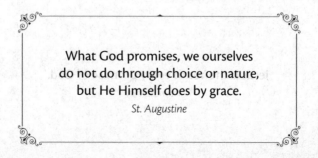

What God promises, we ourselves
do not do through choice or nature,
but He Himself does by grace.

St. Augustine

Many are the plans in a person's heart,
but it is the LORD's purpose that prevails.

Prov. 19:21 NIV

You do not know what tomorrow will bring. What
is your life? For you are a mist that appears for a little
time and then vanishes. Instead you ought to say,
"If the Lord wills, we will live and do this or that."

James 4:14-15 ESV

"Seek the Kingdom of God above all else, and live
righteously, and He will give you everything you need."

Matt. 6:33 NLT

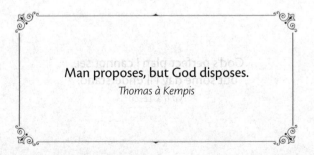

Man proposes, but God disposes.
Thomas à Kempis

"I have a plan for the whole earth," says the Lord.
Isa. 14:26 NLT

My goal is that they may have the full riches of complete
understanding, in order that they may know the
mystery of God, namely, Christ, in whom are
hidden all the treasures of wisdom and knowledge.
Col. 2:2-3 NIV

God wants everyone to be saved
and to know the whole truth.
1 Tim. 2:3-4 CEV

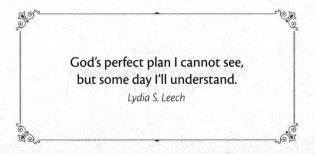

God's perfect plan I cannot see,
but some day I'll understand.

Lydia S. Leech

*All this also comes from the Lord Almighty, whose
plan is wonderful, whose wisdom is magnificent.*
Isa. 28:29 NIV

*If any of you lacks wisdom, let him ask God,
who gives generously to all without reproach,
and it will be given him.*
James 1:5 ESV

*Wisdom belongs to the aged, and understanding
to the old. But true wisdom and power are
found in God; counsel and understanding are His.*
Job 12:12-13 NLT

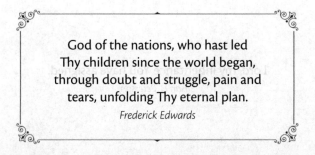

God of the nations, who hast led
Thy children since the world began,
through doubt and struggle, pain and
tears, unfolding Thy eternal plan.
Frederick Edwards

*Because we are united with Christ, we
have received an inheritance from God,
for He chose us in advance, and He makes
everything work out according to His plan.*
Eph. 1:11 NLT

*Commit your work to the LORD,
and your plans will be established.*
Prov. 16:3 ESV

*The righteous will inherit the land
and dwell in it forever.*
Ps. 37:29 NIV

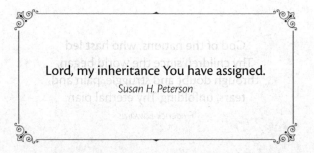

Lord, my inheritance You have assigned.
Susan H. Peterson

God saved us and called us to live a holy life.
He did this, not because we deserved it, but because
that was His plan from before the beginning
of time – to show us His grace through Christ Jesus.

2 Tim. 1:9 NLT

It is because of Him that you are in Christ Jesus,
who has become for us wisdom from God –
that is, our righteousness, holiness and redemption.

1 Cor. 1:30 NIV

Let the message about Christ
completely fill your lives,
while you use all your wisdom
to teach and instruct each other.

Col. 3:16 CEV

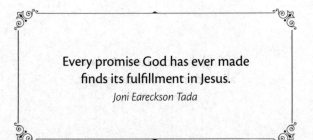

Every promise God has ever made
finds its fulfillment in Jesus.

Joni Eareckson Tada

*For the L*ORD* gives wisdom; from His mouth*
come knowledge and understanding.
Prov. 2:6 ESV

*Respect and obey the L*ORD*!*
This is the beginning of wisdom.
To have understanding,
you must know the Holy God.
Prov. 9:10 CEV

Don't act thoughtlessly,
but understand what the
Lord wants you to do.
Eph. 5:17 NLT

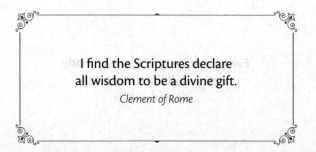

I find the Scriptures declare
all wisdom to be a divine gift.
Clement of Rome

Respect and obey the Lord! This is the
first step to wisdom and good sense.
Ps. 111:10 CEV

And so, my children, listen to me,
for all who follow my ways are joyful.
Listen to my instruction and be wise.
Don't ignore it.
Prov. 8:32-33 NLT

"Therefore everyone who hears these words
of Mine and puts them into practice is like
a wise man who built his house on the rock."
Matt. 7:24 NIV

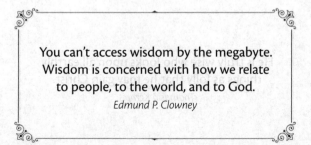

You can't access wisdom by the megabyte.
Wisdom is concerned with how we relate
to people, to the world, and to God.
Edmund P. Clowney

The wisdom that comes from heaven is first of all pure;
then peace-loving, considerate, submissive,
full of mercy and good fruit, impartial and sincere.

James 3:17 NIV

Wisdom will multiply your days
and add years to your life.

Prov. 9:11 NLT

Wisdom will protect you just like money;
knowledge with good sense will lead you to life.

Eccles. 7:12 CEV

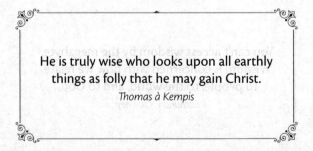

He is truly wise who looks upon all earthly
things as folly that he may gain Christ.

Thomas à Kempis

If any of you lacks wisdom, let him ask God,
who gives generously to all without reproach.
James 1:5 ESV

"I will give you the right words and such
wisdom that none of your opponents
will be able to reply or refute you!"
Luke 21:15 NLT

In Him we have redemption through His blood,
the forgiveness of sins, in accordance with the
riches of God's grace that He lavished on us.
With all wisdom and understanding.
Eph. 1:7-8 NIV

Bliss He wakes, and woe He lightens:
God is wisdom, God is love.
John Bowring

~ JUNE 22 ~

The LORD's teachings last forever,
and they give wisdom to ordinary people.
Ps. 19:7 CEV

Instruct the wise, and they will be even wiser.
Teach the righteous, and they will learn even more.
Prov. 9:9 NLT

"I will instruct you and teach you in the
way you should go; I will counsel
you with My loving eye on you."
Ps. 32:8 NIV

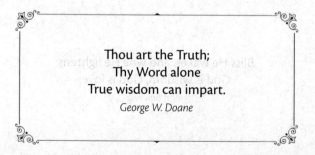

Thou art the Truth;
Thy Word alone
True wisdom can impart.
George W. Doane

*God gives wisdom to the wise and
knowledge to the discerning.*

Dan. 2:21 NIV

*Don't turn your back on wisdom,
for she will protect you.
Love her, and she will guard you.*

Prov. 4:6 NLT

*Behold, You delight in truth in the inward being,
and You teach me wisdom in the secret heart.*

Ps. 51:6 ESV

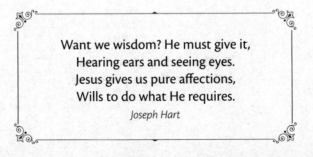

Want we wisdom? He must give it,
Hearing ears and seeing eyes.
Jesus gives us pure affections,
Wills to do what He requires.

Joseph Hart

To the person who pleases Him,
God gives wisdom.
Eccles. 2:26 NIV

Those who obey him will not be punished.
Those who are wise will find a time
and a way to do what is right.
Eccles. 8:5 NLT

You are the foundation on which we stand today.
You always save us and give true wisdom and knowledge.
Nothing means more to us than obeying You.
Isa. 33:6 CEV

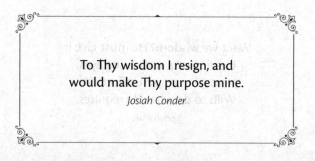

To Thy wisdom I resign, and
would make Thy purpose mine.
Josiah Conder

With God are wisdom and might;
He has counsel and understanding.
Job 12:13 ESV

Trust in the LORD with all your heart
and lean not on your own understanding.
Prov. 3:5 NIV

Then, because you belong to Christ Jesus,
God will bless you with peace that no one
can completely understand. And this peace
will control the way you think and feel.
Phil. 4:7 CEV

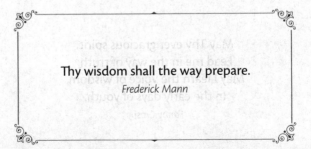

Thy wisdom shall the way prepare.
Frederick Mann

God alone understands the way to wisdom;
He knows where it can be found.
Job 28:23 NLT

By His wisdom and knowledge
the Lord created heaven and earth.
Prov. 3:19 CEV

We know also that the Son of God has
come and has given us understanding,
so that we may know Him who is true.
1 John 5:20 NIV

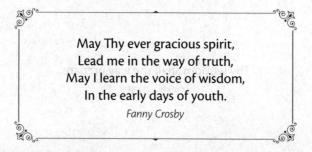

May Thy ever gracious spirit,
Lead me in the way of truth,
May I learn the voice of wisdom,
In the early days of youth.

Fanny Crosby

Blessed are those who find wisdom,
those who gain understanding.
Prov. 3:13 NIV

He has showered His kindness on us,
along with all wisdom and understanding.
Eph. 1:8 NLT

Whoever is wise, let him understand these things;
whoever is discerning, let him know them; for the
ways of the LORD are right, and the upright walk
in them, but transgressors stumble in them.
Hos. 14:9 ESV

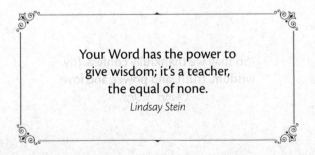

Your Word has the power to
give wisdom; it's a teacher,
the equal of none.
Lindsay Stein

Wisdom is like honey for your life –
if you find it, your future is bright.
Prov. 24:14 CEV

An intelligent heart acquires knowledge,
and the ear of the wise seeks knowledge.
Prov. 18:15 ESV

Wisdom offers you long life ... riches and honor.
She will guide you down delightful paths.
Prov. 3:16-17 NLT

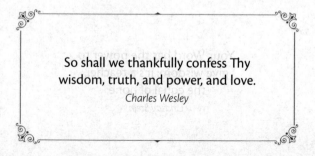

So shall we thankfully confess Thy
wisdom, truth, and power, and love.
Charles Wesley

I thank and praise You, God of my ancestors:
You have given me wisdom and power.
Dan. 2:23 NIV

For those who find Me, find life and
receive favor from the LORD.
Prov. 8:35 NIV

Understanding Your word brings light
to the minds of ordinary people.
Ps. 119:130 CEV

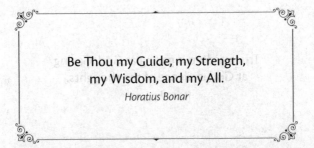

Be Thou my Guide, my Strength,
my Wisdom, and my All.
Horatius Bonar

*I keep asking that the God of our Lord Jesus Christ,
the glorious Father, may give you the Spirit of wisdom
and revelation, so that you may know Him better.*

Eph. 1:17 NIV

*All wisdom comes from the LORD, and so do
common sense and understanding. God gives
helpful advice to everyone who obeys Him and
protects all of those who live as they should.*

Prov. 2:6-7 CEV

*Whoever is wise, let him attend to these things;
let them consider the steadfast love of the LORD.*

Ps. 107:43 ESV

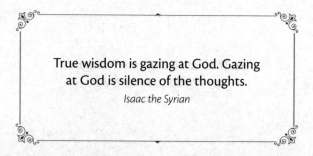

True wisdom is gazing at God. Gazing
at God is silence of the thoughts.

Isaac the Syrian

July

God listens to you and answers your prayers.

The Lord watches over everyone who
obeys Him, and He listens to their prayers.
1 Pet. 3:12 CEV

"If you abide in Me, and My words abide in you,
ask whatever you wish, and it will be done for you."
John 15:7 ESV

"Call to Me and I will answer you and tell you great
and unsearchable things you do not know."
Jer. 33:3 NIV

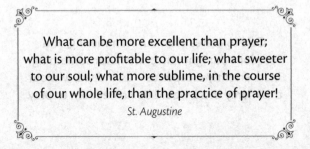

What can be more excellent than prayer;
what is more profitable to our life; what sweeter
to our soul; what more sublime, in the course
of our whole life, than the practice of prayer!

St. Augustine

*If anyone is a worshiper of God and
does His will, God listens to him.*
John 9:31 ESV

*But God did listen! He paid
attention to my prayer.*
Ps. 66:19 NLT

*If I had cherished sin in my heart,
the Lord would not have listened.*
Ps. 66:18 NIV

God tolerates even our stammering, and
pardons our ignorance whenever something
inadvertently escapes us – as, indeed, without
this mercy there would be no freedom to pray.

John Calvin

Know that the Lord has set apart
His faithful servant for Himself;
the Lord hears when I call to Him.

Ps. 4:3 NIV

Don't worry about anything; instead, pray about
everything. Tell God what you need, and thank Him
for all He has done. Then you will experience God's
peace, which exceeds anything we can understand.

Phil. 4:6-7 NLT

"If My people who are called by My name humble
themselves, and pray and seek My face and turn
from their wicked ways, then I will hear from
heaven and will forgive their sin and heal their land."

2 Chron. 7:14 ESV

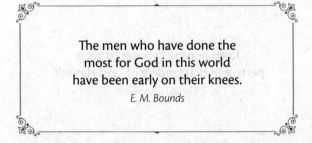

The men who have done the
most for God in this world
have been early on their knees.

E. M. Bounds

When the righteous cry for help,
the Lord hears and delivers
them out of all their troubles.

Ps. 34:17 ESV

You were in serious trouble,
but you prayed to the Lord,
and He rescued you.

Ps. 107:28 CEV

I look to the Lord for help. I wait
confidently for God to save me,
and my God will certainly hear me.

Mic. 7:7 NLT

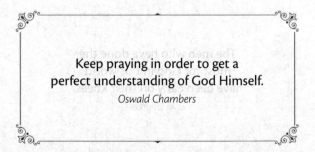

Keep praying in order to get a
perfect understanding of God Himself.

Oswald Chambers

I love the LORD because He hears my voice
and my prayer for mercy. Because He bends
down to listen, I will pray as long as I have breath!
Ps. 116:1-2 NLT

"You will call upon Me and come
and pray to Me, and I will hear you."
Jer. 29:12 ESV

You will pray to Him,
and He will hear you.
Job 22:27 NIV

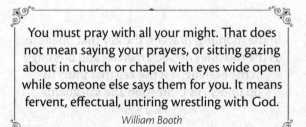

You must pray with all your might. That does
not mean saying your prayers, or sitting gazing
about in church or chapel with eyes wide open
while someone else says them for you. It means
fervent, effectual, untiring wrestling with God.

William Booth

*Morning, noon, and night I cry out in
my distress, and the LORD hears my voice.*

Ps. 55:17 NLT

*In the morning, LORD, You hear my voice;
in the morning I lay my requests
before You and wait expectantly.*

Ps. 5:3 NIV

*The LORD is far from the wicked, but
He hears the prayer of the righteous.*

Prov. 15:29 ESV

In the morning, prayer is the key that opens to
us the treasures of God's mercies and blessings;
in the evening, it is the key that shuts us
up under His protection and safeguard.

Henry Ward Beecher

*I pray to You, God, because You will
help me. Listen and answer my prayer.*
Ps. 17:6 CEV

*When the righteous cry for help, the LORD hears
and delivers them out of all their troubles.*
Ps. 34:17 ESV

*Devote yourselves to prayer with an
alert mind and a thankful heart.*
Col. 4:2 NLT

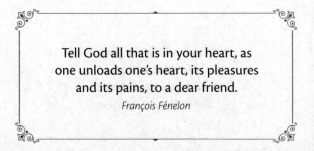

Tell God all that is in your heart, as
one unloads one's heart, its pleasures
and its pains, to a dear friend.
François Fénelon

"I will answer them before they even call to Me.
While they are still talking about their needs,
I will go ahead and answer their prayers!"
Isa. 65:24 NLT

You shall call, and the LORD will answer;
you shall cry, and He will say, "Here I am."
Isa. 58:9 ESV

"They will call upon My name, and I will
answer them. I will say, 'They are My people';
and they will say, 'The LORD is my God.'"
Zech. 13:9 ESV

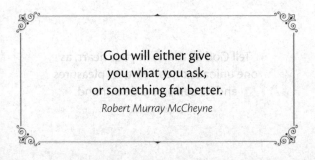

God will either give
you what you ask,
or something far better.
Robert Murray McCheyne

"Call upon Me in the day of trouble;
I will deliver you, and you shall glorify Me."
Ps. 50:15 ESV

"When they call on Me, I will answer;
I will be with them in trouble.
I will rescue and honor them."
Ps. 91:15 NLT

Let them give thanks to the LORD for His unfailing
love and His wonderful deeds for mankind.
Ps. 107:15 NIV

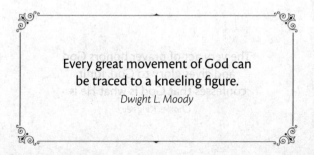

Every great movement of God can
be traced to a kneeling figure.
Dwight L. Moody

*"You will turn back to Me and ask for help,
and I will answer your prayers."*

Jer. 29:12 CEV

"If you ask Me anything in My name, I will do it."

John 14:14 ESV

*We will receive from Him whatever we ask because
we obey Him and do the things that please Him.*

1 John 3:22 NLT

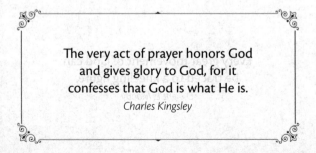

The very act of prayer honors God
and gives glory to God, for it
confesses that God is what He is.

Charles Kingsley

You, LORD, hear the desire of the afflicted;
You encourage them, and You listen to their cry.
Ps. 10:17 NIV

As soon as I pray, You answer me;
You encourage me by giving me strength.
Ps. 138:3 NLT

I waited patiently for the LORD;
He inclined to me and heard my cry.
Ps. 40:1 ESV

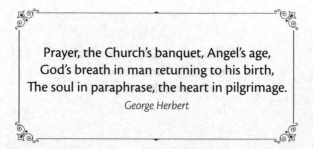

Prayer, the Church's banquet, Angel's age,
God's breath in man returning to his birth,
The soul in paraphrase, the heart in pilgrimage.

George Herbert

You came when I called;
You told me, "Do not fear."
Lam. 3:57 NLT

"If you believe, you will receive
whatever you ask for in prayer."
Matt. 21:22 NIV

Be strong and courageous.
Fear not; do not be dismayed.
1 Chron. 22:13 ESV

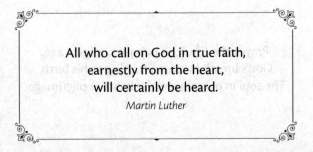

All who call on God in true faith,
earnestly from the heart,
will certainly be heard.

Martin Luther

O Lᴏʀᴅ my God, I cried to You for
help, and You have healed me.
Ps. 30:2 ᴇꜱᴠ

Everyone will come to You
because You answer prayer.
Ps. 65:2 ᴄᴇᴠ

My God will meet all your needs according
to the riches of His glory in Christ Jesus.
Phil. 4:19 ɴɪᴠ

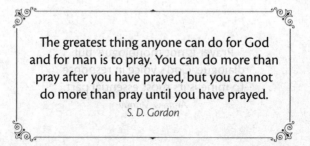

The greatest thing anyone can do for God
and for man is to pray. You can do more than
pray after you have prayed, but you cannot
do more than pray until you have prayed.

S. D. Gordon

*"I have heard your prayer and seen
your tears. I will heal you," says the* LORD.
2 Kings 20:5 NLT

God has heard your prayer.
Acts 10:31 NIV

*We are certain that God will hear our prayers when
we ask for what pleases Him. And if we know
that God listens when we pray, we are sure
that our prayers have already been answered.*
1 John 5:14-15 CEV

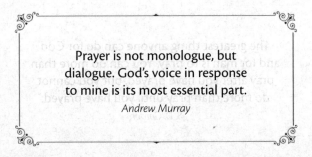

Prayer is not monologue, but
dialogue. God's voice in response
to mine is its most essential part.

Andrew Murray

You will seek the LORD your God and
you will find Him, if you search after Him
with all your heart and with all your soul.

Deut. 4:29 ESV

Look to the LORD and His
strength; seek His face always.

1 Chron. 16:11 NIV

"I love all who love Me. Those
who search will surely find Me."

Prov. 8:17 NLT

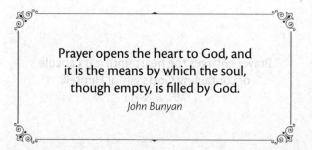

Prayer opens the heart to God, and
it is the means by which the soul,
though empty, is filled by God.

John Bunyan

Seek good, not evil, that you may live.
Then the Lord God Almighty will be with you.
Amos 5:14 NIV

You have said, "Seek my face."
My heart says to you,
"Your face, Lord, do I seek."
Ps. 27:8 ESV

The Lord looks down from heaven on the
entire human race; He looks to see if
anyone is truly wise, if anyone seeks God.
Ps. 14:2 NLT

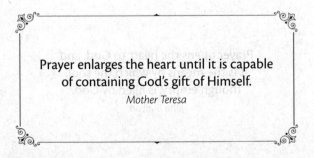

Prayer enlarges the heart until it is capable
of containing God's gift of Himself.
Mother Teresa

"As for me, I would seek God, and to
God would I commit my cause, who
does great things and unsearchable,
marvelous things without number."

Job 5:8-9 ESV

"Ask, and you will receive. Search, and you will find.
Knock, and the door will be opened for you."

Matt. 7:7 CEV

I seek You with all my heart; do not
let me stray from Your commands.

Ps. 119:10 NIV

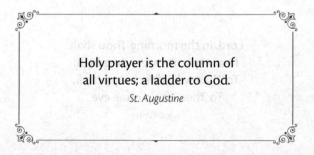

Holy prayer is the column of
all virtues; a ladder to God.

St. Augustine

*The Lord has not despised or scorned
the suffering of the afflicted one;
He has not hidden His face from him
but has listened to his cry for help.*
Ps. 22:24 NIV

*The afflicted shall eat and be satisfied;
those who seek Him shall praise the Lord!
May your hearts live forever!*
Ps. 22:26 ESV

*You listen to the longings of those who suffer.
You offer them hope, and You pay
attention to their cries for help.*
Ps. 10:17 CEV

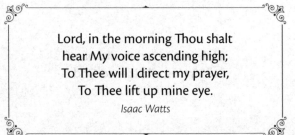

Lord, in the morning Thou shalt
hear My voice ascending high;
To Thee will I direct my prayer,
To Thee lift up mine eye.

Isaac Watts

Those who suffer God delivers in their suffering;
He speaks to them in their affliction.
Job 36:15 NIV

For the needy shall not always be forgotten, and
the hope of the poor shall not perish forever.
Ps. 9:18 ESV

Yet what we suffer now is nothing compared
to the glory He will reveal to us later.
Rom. 8:18 NLT

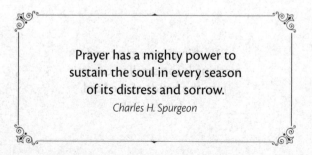

Prayer has a mighty power to
sustain the soul in every season
of its distress and sorrow.

Charles H. Spurgeon

*When we begged our L*ORD *for*
help, He answered our prayer.

Num. 20:16 CEV

Those who know Your name put their trust in You,
*for You, O L*ORD, *have not forsaken those who seek You.*

Ps. 9:10 ESV

"When that time comes, you won't have
to ask Me about anything. I tell you
for certain that the Father will give
you whatever you ask for in My name."

John 16:23 CEV

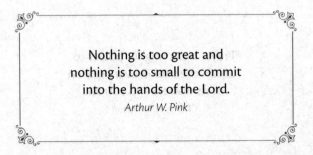

Nothing is too great and
nothing is too small to commit
into the hands of the Lord.

Arthur W. Pink

The LORD answers the prayers of all who obey Him.
Prov. 15:29 CEV

*"If anyone is a worshiper of God and
does His will, God listens to him."*
John 9:31 ESV

*"The people who are really blessed are the
ones who hear and obey God's message!"*
Luke 11:28 CEV

If you keep watch over your hearts,
and listen for the voice of God and
learn of Him, in one short hour you can
learn more from Him than you could
learn from man in a thousand years.

Johannes Tauler

*I was in terrible trouble when I called out
to You, Lord, but from Your temple You
heard me and answered my prayer.*

2 Sam. 22:7 cev

*This poor man cried, and the Lord heard
him and saved him out of all his troubles.*

Ps. 34:6 esv

*The blessing of the Lord makes rich,
and he adds no sorrow with it.*

Prov. 10:22 esv

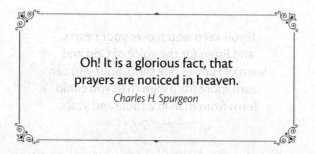

**Oh! It is a glorious fact, that
prayers are noticed in heaven.**

Charles H. Spurgeon

*The LORD has chosen everyone who is faithful
to be His very own, and He answers my prayers.*

Ps. 4:3 CEV

*Faith shows the reality of what we hope for;
it is the evidence of things we cannot see.*

Heb. 11:1 NLT

*"Therefore I tell you, whatever you ask in prayer,
believe that you have received it, and it will be yours."*

Mark 11:24 ESV

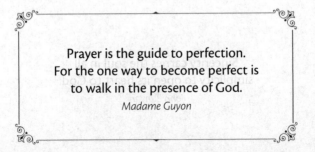

Prayer is the guide to perfection.
For the one way to become perfect is
to walk in the presence of God.

Madame Guyon

*I call on You, my God, for You will answer me;
turn Your ear to me and hear my prayer.*
Ps. 17:6 NIV

I love You, LORD! You answered my prayers.
Ps. 116:1 CEV

*A Prayer of David. Hear a just cause,
O LORD; attend to my cry! Give ear
to my prayer from lips free of deceit!*
Ps. 17:1 ESV

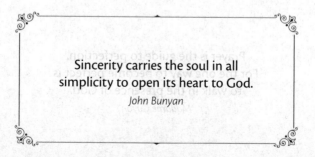

Sincerity carries the soul in all
simplicity to open its heart to God.
John Bunyan

*If you obey the LORD, He will watch
over you and answer your prayers.*

Ps. 34:15 CEV

*You, God, are my God, earnestly I seek You;
I thirst for You, my whole being longs for You.*

Ps. 63:1 NIV

*If one turns away his ear from hearing the law,
even his prayer is an abomination.*

Prov. 28:9 ESV

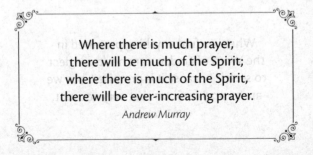

Where there is much prayer,
there will be much of the Spirit;
where there is much of the Spirit,
there will be ever-increasing prayer.

Andrew Murray

Everyone will come to You, God,
because You answer prayer.
Ps. 65:2 CEV

If we know that He hears us in whatever
we ask, we know that we have the
requests that we have asked of Him.
1 John 5:15 ESV

Blessed are those who keep His statutes
and seek Him with all their heart.
Ps. 119:2 NIV

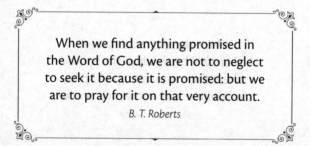

When we find anything promised in
the Word of God, we are not to neglect
to seek it because it is promised: but we
are to pray for it on that very account.

B. T. Roberts

You faithfully answer our prayers
with awesome deeds, O God.
Ps. 65:5 NLT

"When you pray, go into your room, close
the door and pray to your Father, who
is unseen. Then your Father, who sees
what is done in secret, will reward you."
Matt. 6:6 NIV

Praise God, who did not ignore my prayer
or withdraw His unfailing love from me.
Ps. 66:20 NLT

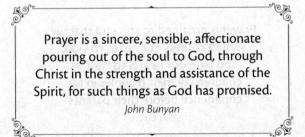

Prayer is a sincere, sensible, affectionate
pouring out of the soul to God, through
Christ in the strength and assistance of the
Spirit, for such things as God has promised.
John Bunyan

When I was really hurting, I prayed to the LORD.
He answered my prayer, and took my worries away.

Ps. 118:5 CEV

He will be gracious if you ask for help. He will
surely respond to the sound of your cries.

Isa. 30:19 NLT

He heals the brokenhearted
and binds up their wounds.

Ps. 147:3 ESV

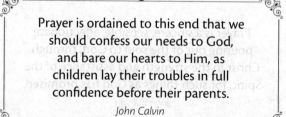

Prayer is ordained to this end that we
should confess our needs to God,
and bare our hearts to Him, as
children lay their troubles in full
confidence before their parents.

John Calvin

*I took my troubles to the LORD; I cried out
to Him, and He answered my prayer.*

Ps. 120:1 NLT

*When you ask, you must believe and not doubt,
because the one who doubts is like a wave
of the sea, blown and tossed by the wind.*

James 1:6 NIV

*Trouble and anguish have found me out,
but Your commandments are my delight.*

Ps. 119:143 ESV

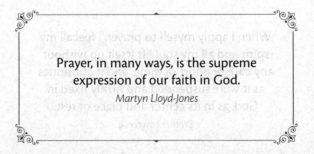

Prayer, in many ways, is the supreme
expression of our faith in God.
Martyn Lloyd-Jones

The Lord hasn't lost His powerful strength;
He can still hear and answer prayers.

Isa. 59:1 CEV

I trust You to save me, Lord God,
and I won't be afraid. My power
and my strength come from You,
and You have saved me.

Isa. 12:2 CEV

Do your best to present yourself to God as one
approved, a worker who has no need to be
ashamed, rightly handling the word of truth.

2 Tim. 2:15 ESV

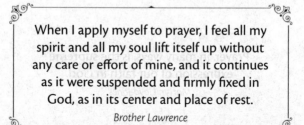

When I apply myself to prayer, I feel all my spirit and all my soul lift itself up without any care or effort of mine, and it continues as it were suspended and firmly fixed in God, as in its center and place of rest.

Brother Lawrence

When I was in trouble, Lord, I prayed to You, and You listened to me. From deep in the world of the dead, I begged for Your help, and You answered my prayer.

Jonah 2:2 CEV

But in my distress I cried out to the Lord; yes, I prayed to my God for help. He heard me from His sanctuary; my cry to Him reached His ears.

Ps. 18:6 NLT

"You must really believe it will happen and have no doubt in your heart. I tell you, you can pray for anything, and if you believe that you've received it, it will be yours."

Mark 11:22-24 NLT

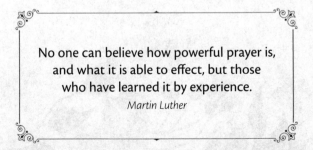

No one can believe how powerful prayer is, and what it is able to effect, but those who have learned it by experience.

Martin Luther

August

God will bless you, reward you and make you prosper.

~ AUGUST 1 ~

I pray that the LORD will bless and protect you,
and that He will show you mercy and kindness.
Num. 6:24-25 CEV

For You bless the righteous, O LORD;
You cover him with favor as with a shield.
Ps. 5:12 ESV

God is able to bless you abundantly,
so that in all things at all times,
having all that you need, you
will abound in every good work.
2 Cor. 9:8 NIV

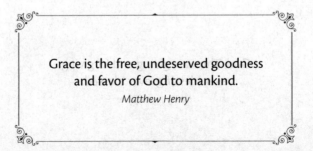

Grace is the free, undeserved goodness
and favor of God to mankind.
Matthew Henry

Blessed are those whose ways are blameless,
who walk according to the law of the LORD.

Ps. 119:1 NIV

"Blessed are the pure in heart,
for they shall see God."

Matt. 5:8 ESV

"I will bless those who trust Me."

Jer. 17:7 CEV

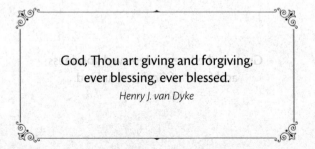

God, Thou art giving and forgiving,
ever blessing, ever blessed.

Henry J. van Dyke

The Lord will send rain at the proper time from His rich treasury in the heavens and will bless all the work you do. You will lend to many nations, but you will never need to borrow from them.

Deut. 28:12 NLT

All the nations of the earth shall be blessed.

Gen. 26:4 ESV

Blessed is the one who does not walk in step with the wicked, but whose delight is in the law of the LORD. That person is like a tree planted by streams of water, which yields its fruit in season and whose leaf does not wither – whatever they do prospers.

Ps. 1:1-3 NIV

God desires us to understand that, when He blesses us, it is not to simply make us happy, but so that we would still further communicate His blessing. God Himself is love, and therefore He blesses.

Andrew Murray

"The people who are really blessed are the
ones who hear and obey God's message!"
Luke 11:28 CEV

Blessed are all who fear the LORD,
who walk in obedience to Him.
You will eat the fruit of your labor;
blessings and prosperity will be yours.
Ps. 128:1-2 NIV

"I will be with you and will bless you."
Gen. 26:3 ESV

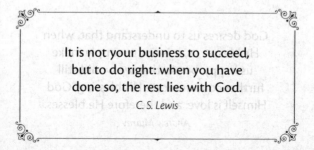

It is not your business to succeed,
but to do right: when you have
done so, the rest lies with God.
C. S. Lewis

LORD, You alone are my inheritance, my cup of blessing.
You guard all that is mine. The land You have given
me is a pleasant land. What a wonderful inheritance!

Ps. 16:5-6 NLT

"I will provide grass in the fields for your
cattle, and you will eat and be satisfied."

Deut. 11:15 NIV

God will take care of all your needs with the
wonderful blessings that come from Christ Jesus!

Phil. 4:19 CEV

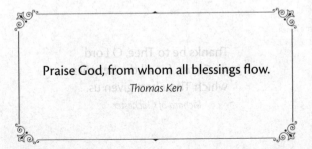

Praise God, from whom all blessings flow.

Thomas Ken

*Oh, taste and see that the L*ORD *is good!*
Blessed is the man who takes refuge in Him!

Ps. 34:8 ESV

"Seek the kingdom of God above
all else, and live righteously, and
He will give you everything you need."

Matt. 6:33 NLT

*The L*ORD *is my Shepherd,*
I lack nothing. He leads
me beside quiet waters,
He refreshes my soul.

Ps. 23:1-3 NIV

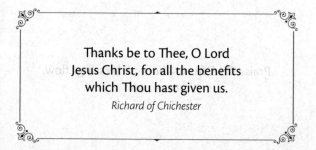

Thanks be to Thee, O Lord
Jesus Christ, for all the benefits
which Thou hast given us.

Richard of Chichester

There truly is a reward for those who live for God.
Ps. 58:11 NLT

Blessings are on the head of the righteous.
Prov. 10:6 ESV

Remember that the Lord will reward
each one of us for the good we do.
Eph. 6:8 NLT

When thou has truly thanked the
Lord for every blessing sent,
but little time will then remain
for murmur or lament.

Hannah More

If you obey God's commands,
you will be rewarded.
Prov. 13:13 CEV

If they obey and serve Him, they will
spend the rest of their days in prosperity
and their years in contentment.
Job 36:11 NIV

Therefore, obey the terms of this covenant
so that you will prosper in everything you do.
Deut. 29:9 NLT

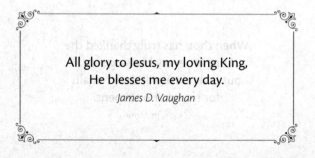

All glory to Jesus, my loving King,
He blesses me every day.
James D. Vaughan

Tell those who obey God, "You're very fortunate –
you will be rewarded for what you have done."

Isa. 3:10 CEV

"Give, and it will be given to you. A good measure,
pressed down, shaken together and running over,
will be poured into your lap. For with the
measure you use, it will be measured to you."

Luke 6:38 NIV

"When you give to someone in need, don't let your
left hand know what your right hand is doing.
Give your gifts in private, and your Father,
who sees everything, will reward you."

Matt. 6:3-4 NLT

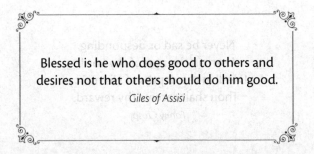

Blessed is he who does good to others and
desires not that others should do him good.

Giles of Assisi

God will reward each of us for
what we have done.

Rom. 2:6 CEV

For those blessed by the LORD shall inherit the land.
Ps. 37:22 ESV

"Restrain your voice from weeping
and your eyes from tears,
for your work will be rewarded,"
declares the LORD.

Jer. 31:16 NIV

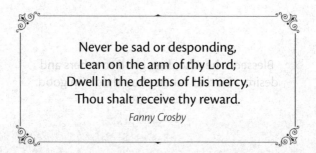

Never be sad or desponding,
Lean on the arm of thy Lord;
Dwell in the depths of His mercy,
Thou shalt receive thy reward.

Fanny Crosby

*God will bless you, if you don't give
up when your faith is being tested.
He will reward you with a glorious life,
just as He rewards everyone who loves Him.*

James 1:12 CEV

*As for you, be strong and do not give up,
for your work will be rewarded.*

2 Chron. 15:7 NIV

*May the LORD give strength to His people!
May the LORD bless His people with peace!*

Ps. 29:11 ESV

God is more anxious to
bestow His blessings on us
than we are to receive them.

St. Augustine

Whoever is kind to the poor lends to the LORD,
and He will reward them for what they have done.
Prov. 19:17 NIV

"God blesses those who are humble,
for they will inherit the whole earth."
Matt. 5:5 NLT

From the fruit of his mouth a man is satisfied with good,
and the work of a man's hand comes back to him.
Prov. 12:14 ESV

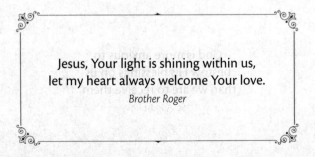

Jesus, Your light is shining within us,
let my heart always welcome Your love.
Brother Roger

"For I, the LORD, love justice; I hate robbery and wrongdoing. In My faithfulness I will reward My people and make an everlasting covenant with them."

Isa. 61:8 NIV

You shall remember the LORD your God, for it is He who gives you power to get wealth, that He may confirm His covenant that He swore to your fathers, as it is this day.

Deut. 8:18 ESV

The LORD rewarded me for doing right; He restored me because of my innocence.

Ps. 18:20 NLT

Never tire of doing good;
someday there'll be reward.

Susan H. Peterson

I leave it all in the LORD's hand;
I will trust God for my reward.

Isa. 49:4 NLT

Honor the LORD with your wealth,
with the first fruits of all your crops;
then your barns will be filled to overflowing,
and your vats will brim over with new wine.

Prov. 3:9-10 NIV

Because of all that the Son is, we have
been given one blessing after another.

John 1:16 CEV

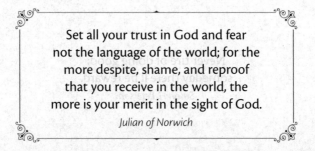

Set all your trust in God and fear
not the language of the world; for the
more despite, shame, and reproof
that you receive in the world, the
more is your merit in the sight of God.

Julian of Norwich

*Stay on the path that the L*ORD* your*
God has commanded you to follow.
Then you will live long and prosperous lives.

Deut. 5:33 NLT

*The L*ORD* blesses the dwelling of the righteous.*

Prov. 3:33 ESV

"Have I not commanded you? Be strong
and courageous. Do not be afraid;
*do not be discouraged, for the L*ORD* your*
God will be with you wherever you go."

Josh. 1:9 NIV

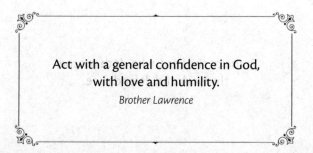

Act with a general confidence in God,
with love and humility.

Brother Lawrence

Trust in the LORD and do good. Then you will live safely in the land and prosper.

Ps. 37:3 NLT

The LORD your God will make you abundantly prosperous in all the work of your hand.

Deut. 30:9 ESV

For the LORD your God will bless you in all your harvest and in all the work of your hands, and your joy will be complete.

Deut. 16:15 NIV

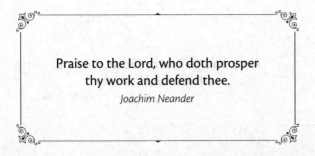

Praise to the Lord, who doth prosper thy work and defend thee.

Joachim Neander

God's people will prosper like healthy plants.

Prov. 11:28 CEV

Let the favor of the Lord our God be
upon us, and establish the work
of our hands upon us; yes,
establish the work of our hands!

Ps. 90:17 ESV

Blessings and prosperity will be yours.

Ps. 128:2 NIV

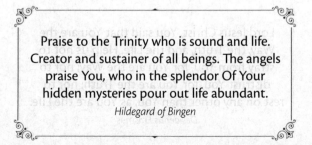

Praise to the Trinity who is sound and life.
Creator and sustainer of all beings. The angels
praise You, who in the splendor Of Your
hidden mysteries pour out life abundant.

Hildegard of Bingen

*Those who trust in the L*ORD *will prosper.*
Prov. 28:25 NIV

"Blessed are those who have
not seen and yet have believed."
John 20:29 ESV

*Oh, the joys of those who trust the L*ORD*,*
who have no confidence in the
proud or in those who worship idols.
Ps. 40:4 NLT

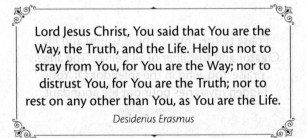

Lord Jesus Christ, You said that You are the
Way, the Truth, and the Life. Help us not to
stray from You, for You are the Way; nor to
distrust You, for You are the Truth; nor to
rest on any other than You, as You are the Life.

Desiderius Erasmus

AUGUST 19

Everyone who lives right and
respects God will prosper.

Eccles. 8:12 CEV

The generation of the
upright will be blessed.

Ps. 112:2 NIV

The God of heaven will
make us prosper.

Neh. 2:20 ESV

Blessed is the Pilgrim who seeketh not an abiding place unto himself in this world; but longeth to be dissolved, and be with Christ in heaven.

Thomas à Kempis

*You will prosper if you are careful to observe the
statutes and the rules that the Lord commanded.*

1 Chron. 22:13 ESV

*The Lord blesses everyone
who worships Him and
gladly obeys His teachings.*

Ps. 112:1 CEV

*"I the Lord search the heart and examine the mind,
to reward each person according to their conduct,
according to what their deeds deserve."*

Jer. 17:10 NIV

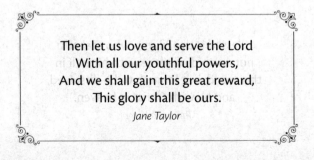

Then let us love and serve the Lord
With all our youthful powers,
And we shall gain this great reward,
This glory shall be ours.

Jane Taylor

The LORD is like a father to His children,
tender and compassionate.
Ps. 103:13 NLT

For the LORD God is a sun and shield;
the LORD bestows favor and honor.
Ps. 84:11 NIV

Bless the LORD, O my soul,
and forget not all His benefits.
Ps. 103:2 ESV

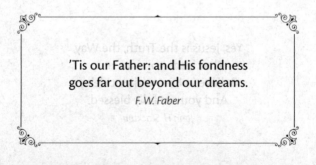

'Tis our Father: and His fondness
goes far out beyond our dreams.
F. W. Faber

*Continue to fear the L*ORD.
You will be rewarded for this;
your hope will not be disappointed.
Prov. 23:17-18 NLT

*Whoever fears the L*ORD *has a secure fortress,*
and for their children it will be a refuge.
Prov. 14:26 NIV

*The fear of the L*ORD *leads to life,*
and whoever has it rests satisfied.
Prov. 19:23 ESV

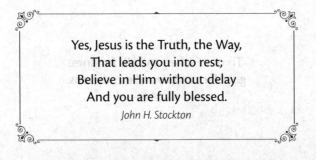

Yes, Jesus is the Truth, the Way,
That leads you into rest;
Believe in Him without delay
And you are fully blessed.

John H. Stockton

AUGUST 23

*The Lord God of Jacob blesses everyone
who trusts Him and depends on Him.*

Ps. 146:5 CEV

*"Blessed is the man who trusts in
the Lord, whose trust is the Lord."*

Jer. 17:7 ESV

*Trust in the Lord forever, for the Lord,
the Lord Himself, is the Rock eternal.*

Isa. 26:4 NIV

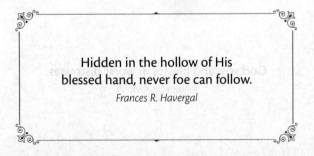

Hidden in the hollow of His
blessed hand, never foe can follow.

Frances R. Havergal

"God blesses those people who depend only on Him.
They belong to the kingdom of heaven!"

Matt. 5:3 CEV

"But seek first the kingdom of God and His righteousness,
and all these things will be added to you."

Matt. 6:33 ESV

The LORD rewards everyone for their
righteousness and faithfulness.

1 Sam. 26:23 NIV

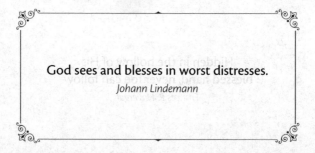

God sees and blesses in worst distresses.
Johann Lindemann

*You bless those people who are
honest and fair in everything they do.*

Ps. 106:3 CEV

*For the LORD is a God of justice.
Blessed are all who wait for Him!*

Isa. 30:18 NIV

*The one who looks into the perfect law,
the law of liberty, and perseveres, being
no hearer who forgets but a doer who acts,
he will be blessed in his doing.*

James 1:25 ESV

The blessing of the Lord rest and
remain upon all His people, in every
land and of every tongue; the Lord
meet in mercy all who seek Him.

Handley Moule

The LORD satisfies your desires with good things
so that your youth is renewed like the eagle's.
Ps. 103:5 NIV

You make known to me the path of life;
in Your presence there is fullness of joy; at
Your right hand are pleasures forevermore.
Ps. 16:11 ESV

When God gives someone wealth and possessions,
and the ability to enjoy them, to accept their lot
and be happy in their toil – this is a gift of God.
Eccles. 5:19 NIV

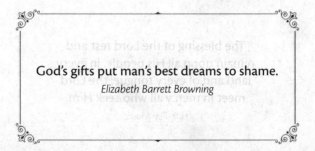

God's gifts put man's best dreams to shame.
Elizabeth Barrett Browning

"God blesses those people who make peace.
They will be called His children."

Matt. 5:9 CEV

Blessed is he who comes in the name of the LORD!
We bless you from the house of the LORD.

Ps. 118:26 ESV

Blessed are those who keep His statutes
and seek Him with all their heart.

Ps. 119:2 NIV

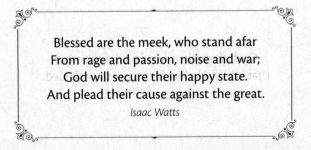

Blessed are the meek, who stand afar
From rage and passion, noise and war;
God will secure their happy state.
And plead their cause against the great.

Isaac Watts

Submit to God and be at peace with Him;
in this way prosperity will come to you.
Job 22:21 NIV

In the day of prosperity be joyful.
Eccles. 7:14 ESV

Let the peace that comes from Christ rule in your
hearts. For as members of one body you are
called to live in peace. And always be thankful.
Col. 3:15 NLT

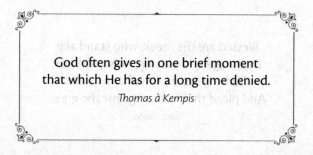

God often gives in one brief moment
that which He has for a long time denied.

Thomas à Kempis

When God blesses His people, their city prospers.

Prov. 11:11 CEV

The blessing of the Lord makes rich,
and He adds no sorrow with it.

Prov. 10:22 ESV

Praise be to the God and Father of our Lord
Jesus Christ, who has blessed us in the heavenly
realms with every spiritual blessing in Christ.

Eph. 1:3 NIV

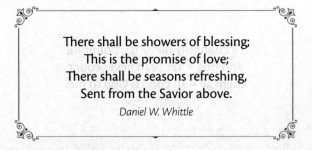

There shall be showers of blessing;
This is the promise of love;
There shall be seasons refreshing,
Sent from the Savior above.

Daniel W. Whittle

If you know what you're doing, you will prosper.
God blesses everyone who trusts Him.
Prov. 16:20 CEV

Good planning and hard work lead to prosperity.
Prov. 21:5 NLT

May the God of hope fill you with
all joy and peace in believing,
so that by the power of the
Holy Spirit you may abound in hope.
Rom. 15:13 ESV

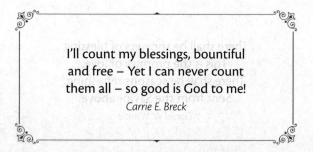

I'll count my blessings, bountiful
and free – Yet I can never count
them all – so good is God to me!
Carrie E. Breck

Because of Christ there are blessings
that cannot be measured.
Eph. 3:8 CEV

"Rejoice and be glad, for your reward is great in heaven."
Matt. 5:12 ESV

"I will open the windows of heaven for you.
I will pour out a blessing so great you
won't have enough room to take it in.
Try it! Put Me to the test!"
Mal. 3:10 NLT

Count your blessings, name them one by one,
Count your blessings, see what God hath done!
Count your blessings, name them one by one,
And it will surprise you what the Lord hath done.

Johnson Oatman Jr.

September

God is your confidence,
strength and salvation.

"Blessed are those who trust in the LORD and
have made the LORD their hope and confidence."
Jer. 17:7 NLT

The LORD will be your confidence and
will keep your foot from being caught.
Prov. 3:26 NIV

The law never made anything perfect.
But now we have confidence in a better hope,
through which we draw near to God.
Heb. 7:19 NLT

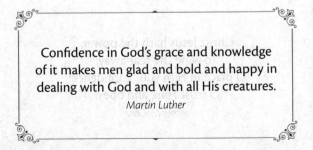

Confidence in God's grace and knowledge
of it makes men glad and bold and happy in
dealing with God and with all His creatures.
Martin Luther

We have placed our confidence in Him,
and He will continue to rescue us.
2 Cor. 1:10 NLT

Christ now gives us courage and confidence,
so that we can come to God by faith.
Eph. 3:12 CEV

The fruit of that righteousness will be peace;
its effect will be quietness and confidence forever.
Isa. 32:17 NIV

Christ Jesus hath the power,
To wipe the tear away;
O place in Him your confidence!
O trust Him, and obey!

James M. Gray

*We can say with confidence, "The LORD
is my helper, so I will have no fear."*
Heb. 13:6 NLT

*This is the confidence that we have toward Him, that
if we ask anything according to His will He hears us.*
1 John 5:14 ESV

*Now to Him who is able to do immeasurably
more than all we ask or imagine, according
to His power that is at work within us, to
Him be glory in the church and in Christ Jesus
throughout all generations, for ever and ever!*
Eph. 3:20-21 NIV

A cheerful confidence I feel,
My well-placed hopes with joy I see;
My bosom glows with heav'nly zeal
To worship Him who died for me.

William Cowper

Let us then with confidence draw near
to the throne of grace, that we may receive
mercy and find grace to help in time of need.
Heb. 4:16 ESV

"My grace is all you need.
My power works best in weakness."
2 Cor. 12:9 NLT

Being confident of this, that He who began
a good work in you will carry it on to
completion until the day of Christ Jesus.
Phil. 1:6 NIV

My God is reconciled; His pardoning voice
I hear; He owns me for His child; I can no
longer fear: With confidence I now draw
nigh. And "Father, Abba, Father," cry.

Charles Wesley

Such is the confidence that we have through
Christ toward God. Not that we are sufficient
in ourselves to claim anything as coming
from us, but our sufficiency is from God.
2 Cor. 3:4-5 ESV

Let us who live in the light be clearheaded, protected
by the armor of faith and love, and wearing as
our helmet the confidence of our salvation.
1 Thess. 5:8 NLT

Since we have been justified through faith, we have
peace with God through our Lord Jesus Christ.
Rom. 5:1 NIV

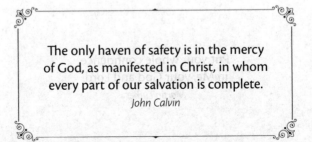

The only haven of safety is in the mercy
of God, as manifested in Christ, in whom
every part of our salvation is complete.
John Calvin

You have been my hope, Sovereign LORD,
my confidence since my youth.

Ps. 71:5 NIV

It is better to trust the LORD for
protection than to trust anyone else.

Ps. 118:8 CEV

By awesome deeds You answer us with
righteousness, O God of our salvation, the hope of
all the ends of the earth and of the farthest seas.

Ps. 65:5 ESV

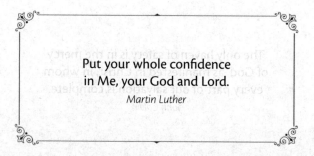

**Put your whole confidence
in Me, your God and Lord.**
Martin Luther

God is our refuge and strength,
an ever-present help in trouble.

Ps. 46:1 NIV

The LORD is my strength and my
song; He has given me victory.

Ps. 118:14 NLT

The LORD gives strength to those who are weary.

Isa. 40:29 CEV

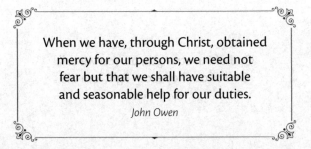

When we have, through Christ, obtained
mercy for our persons, we need not
fear but that we shall have suitable
and seasonable help for our duties.

John Owen

The Sovereign LORD is my strength!
He makes me as surefooted as a deer,
able to tread upon the heights.
Hab. 3:19 NLT

Ah, LORD God! It is You who have made the heavens
and the earth by Your great power and by Your
outstretched arm! Nothing is too hard for You.
Jer. 32:17 ESV

It is God who arms me with strength and keeps
my way secure. He makes my feet like the feet
of a deer; He causes me to stand on the heights.
2 Sam. 22:33-34 NIV

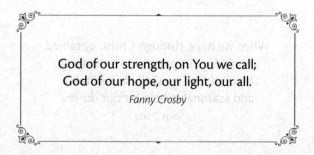

God of our strength, on You we call;
God of our hope, our light, our all.
Fanny Crosby

The LORD is my strength and my shield; in Him my heart trusts, and I am helped; my heart exults, and with my song I give thanks to Him.

Ps. 28:7 ESV

I thank and praise You, God of my ancestors, for You have given me wisdom and strength.

Dan. 2:23 NLT

Splendor and majesty are before Him; strength and joy are in His dwelling place.

1 Chron. 16:27 NIV

O God, my strength and fortitude
In truth I will love Thee;
Thou art my castle and
defense In my necessity.
Thomas Sternhold

I can do all things through Him who strengthens me.
Phil. 4:13 ESV

Be strong in the Lord and in His mighty power.
Eph. 6:10 NIV

May our Lord Jesus Christ, who loved us,
strengthen you in every good thing you do and say.
2 Thess. 2:16-17 NLT

In God alone there is faithfulness and
faith in the trust that we may hold to Him,
to His promise and to His guidance. To hold
to God is to rely on the fact that God is
there for me, and to live in this certainty.

Karl Barth

But those who trust the LORD will find new strength.
They will be strong like eagles soaring upward on wings;
they will walk and run without getting tired.

Isa. 40:31 CEV

In Your strength I can crush an army;
with my God I can scale any wall.

Ps. 18:29 NLT

"In repentance and rest is your salvation,
in quietness and trust is your strength."

Isa. 30:15 NIV

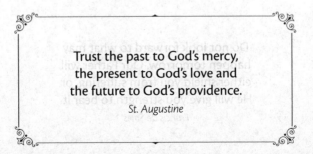

Trust the past to God's mercy,
the present to God's love and
the future to God's providence.

St. Augustine

"Do not be grieved, for the joy of
the LORD is your strength."
Neh. 8:10 ESV

"I will search for My lost ones, and I will bring
them safely home again. I will bandage
the injured and strengthen the weak."
Ezek. 34:16 NLT

My flesh and my heart may fail,
but God is the strength of my
heart and my portion forever.
Ps. 73:26 NIV

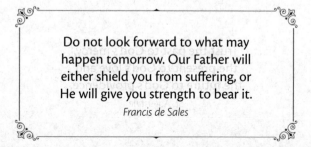

Do not look forward to what may
happen tomorrow. Our Father will
either shield you from suffering, or
He will give you strength to bear it.

Francis de Sales

The LORD lives! Praise to my Rock!
May the God of my salvation be exalted!
Ps. 18:46 NLT

Oh sing to the LORD a new song; sing to the
LORD, all the earth! Sing to the LORD, bless
His name; tell of His salvation from day to day.
Declare His glory among the nations,
His marvelous works among all the peoples!
Ps. 96:1-3 ESV

Restore to me the joy of Your salvation and
grant me a willing spirit, to sustain me.
Ps. 51:12 NIV

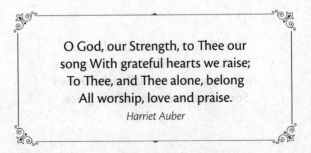

O God, our Strength, to Thee our
song With grateful hearts we raise;
To Thee, and Thee alone, belong
All worship, love and praise.

Harriet Auber

The LORD gives His people strength.
The LORD blesses them with peace.

Ps. 29:11 NLT

The LORD is good, a refuge in times of trouble.
He cares for those who trust in Him.

Nah. 1:7 NIV

The way of the LORD is a stronghold to
the blameless, but destruction to evildoers.

Prov. 10:29 ESV

Thus far the Lord hath led me on,
Thus far His power prolongs my days,
And every evening shall make known
Some fresh memorial of His grace.

Isaac Watts

The LORD is my strength and my song;
He has given me victory. This is
my God, and I will praise Him – my
father's God, and I will exalt Him!

Exod. 15:2 NLT

Yours, LORD, is the greatness and the power
and the glory and the majesty and the
splendor, for everything in heaven and
earth is Yours. Yours, LORD, is the Kingdom;
you are exalted as head over all.

1 Chron. 29:11 NIV

"Fear not, for I am with you; be not dismayed, for I am
your God; I will strengthen you, I will help you."

Isa. 41:10 ESV

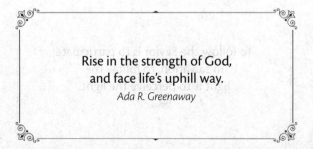

Rise in the strength of God,
and face life's uphill way.

Ada R. Greenaway

On God rests my salvation.
Ps. 62:7 ESV

If we are living in the light, as God is in the light,
then we have fellowship with each other, and
the blood of Jesus, His Son, cleanses us from all sin.
1 John 1:7 NLT

Christ never sinned! But God treated him as a sinner,
so that Christ could make us acceptable to God.
2 Cor. 5:21 CEV

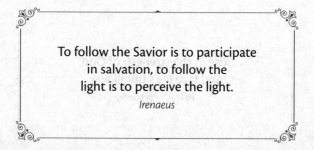

To follow the Savior is to participate
in salvation, to follow the
light is to perceive the light.
Irenaeus

Our God is a God of salvation.
Ps. 68:20 ESV

*If we confess our sins to Him, He is
faithful and just to forgive us our sins
and to cleanse us from all wickedness.*
1 John 1:9 NLT

*Anyone who belongs to Christ is a new person.
The past is forgotten, and everything is new.*
2 Cor. 5:17 CEV

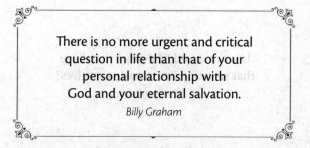

There is no more urgent and critical
question in life than that of your
personal relationship with
God and your eternal salvation.

Billy Graham

We are surrounded by the walls of God's salvation.

Isa. 26:1 NLT

For the LORD takes pleasure in His people;
He adorns the humble with salvation.

Ps. 149:4 ESV

Children, I am writing you, because your sins
have been forgiven in the name of Christ.

1 John 2:12 CEV

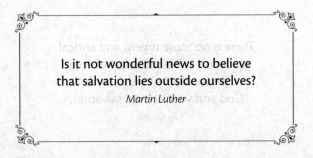

Is it not wonderful news to believe
that salvation lies outside ourselves?

Martin Luther

"Let all the world look to Me for salvation!
For I am God; there is no other."
Isa. 45:22 NLT

"Seek Me and live."
Amos 5:4 ESV

If from there you seek the LORD your God,
you will find Him if you seek Him with
all your heart and with all your soul.
Deut. 4:29 NIV

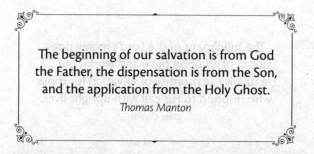

The beginning of our salvation is from God
the Father, the dispensation is from the Son,
and the application from the Holy Ghost.
Thomas Manton

The salvation of the righteous comes from the L<small>ORD</small>.
Ps. 37:39 NIV

"The L<small>ORD</small> God is kind and merciful,
and if you turn back to Him, He
will no longer turn His back on you."
2 Chron. 30:9 CEV

The way of the L<small>ORD</small> is a stronghold
to those with integrity,
but it destroys the wicked.
Prov. 10:29 NLT

The fulfillment of the Lord's mercy does
not depend upon believers' works, but ...
He fulfills the promise of salvation for those
who respond to His call with upright lives.
John Calvin

*It is good to wait quietly for
the salvation of the Lord.*

Lam. 3:26 NIV

*Seek the Lord and His strength;
seek His presence continually!*

1 Chron. 16:11 ESV

*"If you look for Me wholeheartedly,
you will find Me."*

Jer. 29:13 NLT

Seek not to explore the heights
of the divine majesty, but to
find salvation in the saving
deeds of God our Savior.

William of St. Thierry

"It is I, the LORD, announcing your salvation!
It is I, the LORD, who has the power to save!"

Isa. 63:1 NLT

"The gracious hand of our God is
on everyone who looks to Him."

Ezra 8:22 NIV

"Truly, truly, I say to you, whoever hears
My word and believes Him who sent Me
has eternal life. He does not come into
judgment, but has passed from death to life."

John 5:24 ESV

Salvation unto us has come by
God's free grace and favor.

Paul Speratus

God is my King from long ago;
He brings salvation on the earth.

Ps. 74:12 NIV

When God our Savior revealed His kindness and
love, He saved us, not because of the righteous
things we had done, but because of His mercy.
He washed away our sins, giving us a new
birth and new life through the Holy Spirit.
He generously poured out the Spirit
upon us through Jesus Christ our Savior.

Titus 3:4-6 NLT

"They sinned and rebelled against Me, but
I will forgive them and take away their guilt."

Jer. 33:8 CEV

O Thou God of my salvation, my
Redeemer from all sin; Moved by Thy
divine compassion, who hast died my
heart to win; I will praise Thee, I will praise
Thee, where shall I Thy praise begin?

Thomas Olivers

There is salvation in no one else, than Jesus.

Acts 4:12 ESV

God saved you by His grace when you believed. And you can't take credit for this; it is a gift from God. Salvation is not a reward for the good things we have done, so none of us can boast about it.

Eph. 2:8-9 NLT

Christ obeyed God our Father and gave Himself as a sacrifice for our sins to rescue us from this evil world.

Gal. 1:4 CEV

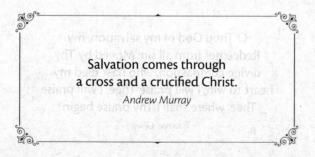

Salvation comes through
a cross and a crucified Christ.

Andrew Murray

*The LORD lives, and blessed be my Rock, and
exalted be my God, the Rock of my salvation.*

2 Sam. 22:47 ESV

*Those who trust in the LORD
will lack no good thing.*

Ps. 34:10 NLT

*As for you, you were dead in
your transgressions and sins.*

Eph. 2:1 NIV

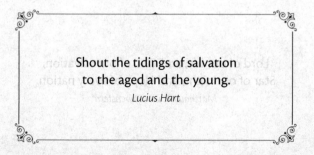

Shout the tidings of salvation
to the aged and the young.

Lucius Hart

Lead me in Your truth and teach me,
for You are the God of my salvation.
Ps. 25:5 ESV

Indeed, this will turn out for my deliverance, for
no godless person would dare come before Him!
Job 13:16 NIV

Turn to God. Then times of refreshment
will come from the presence of the Lord.
Acts 3:19-20 NLT

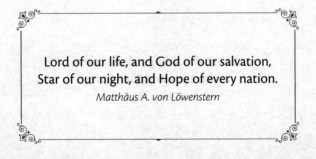

Lord of our life, and God of our salvation,
Star of our night, and Hope of every nation.

Matthäus A. von Löwenstern

Why are you cast down, O my soul,
and why are you in turmoil within me?
Hope in God; for I shall again praise Him,
my Salvation and my God.

Ps. 42:11 ESV

"I will offer sacrifices to you with songs of
praise, and I will fulfill all my vows. For my
salvation comes from the LORD alone."

Jonah 2:9 NLT

I delight greatly in the Lord; my soul rejoices in my God.
For He has clothed me with garments of salvation
and arrayed me in a robe of His righteousness.

Isa. 61:10 NIV

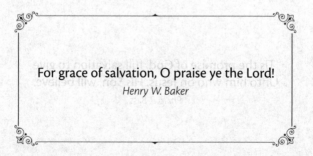

For grace of salvation, O praise ye the Lord!

Henry W. Baker

*I keep praying to You, LORD, hoping this time
You will show me favor. In Your unfailing love,
O God, answer my prayer with Your sure salvation.*

Ps. 69:13 NLT

*Then they cried to the LORD in their trouble,
and He delivered them from their distress.
He sent out His word and healed them,
and delivered them from their destruction.*

Ps. 107:19-20 ESV

*I do not nullify the grace of God, for
if righteousness were through the law,
then Christ died for no purpose.*

Gal. 2:21 ESV

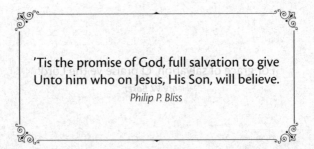

'Tis the promise of God, full salvation to give
Unto him who on Jesus, His Son, will believe.

Philip P. Bliss

*All the ends of the earth have seen
the salvation of our God.*

Ps. 98:3 ESV

*For God did not appoint us to suffer wrath but
to receive salvation through our Lord Jesus Christ.*

1 Thess. 5:9 NIV

*The LORD God, who saves them,
will bless and reward them.*

Ps. 24:5 CEV

Salvation is wholly of the Lord and bears
those signatures of infinite wisdom, power,
and goodness which distinguish all His
works from the puny imitations of men.

John Newton

"God has come to save me. I will trust in Him and not be afraid. The Lord God is my strength and my song; He has given me victory."

Isa. 12:2 ESV

Truly my soul finds rest in God; my salvation comes from Him.

Ps. 62:1 NIV

Salvation belongs to the Lord; Your blessing be on Your people!

Ps. 3:8 ESV

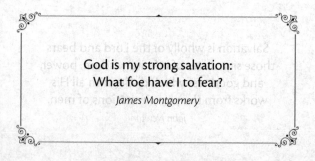

**God is my strong salvation:
What foe have I to fear?**

James Montgomery

October

You can depend on God and He can
be trusted to keep His promises.

OCTOBER 1

All the LORD's promises prove true.
2 Sam. 22:31 NLT

God never tells a lie!
Titus 1:2 CEV

Not one word has failed of all
the good promises He gave.
1 Kings 8:56 NIV

He will keep His word – the gracious One,
full of grace and truth; no doubt of it.

David Livingstone

*No matter how many promises God
has made, they are "Yes" in Christ.*

2 Cor. 1:20 NIV

*He is the faithful God who keeps
His covenant for a thousand generations.*

Deut. 7:9 NLT

He will still be faithful. Christ cannot deny who He is.

2 Tim. 2:13 CEV

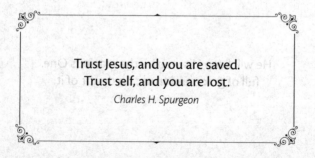

Trust Jesus, and you are saved.
Trust self, and you are lost.

Charles H. Spurgeon

Not one of all the LORD's good promises
to Israel failed; every one was fulfilled.

Josh. 21:45 NIV

"For the promise is for you and for your children
and for all who are far off, everyone
whom the Lord our God calls to himself."

Acts 2:39 ESV

The LORD is righteous in all His
ways and faithful in all He does.

Ps. 145:17 NIV

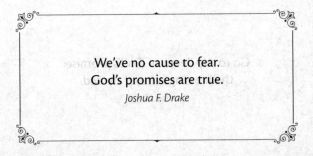

We've no cause to fear.
God's promises are true.

Joshua F. Drake

The LORD's promises are pure,
like silver refined in a furnace,
purified seven times over.
Ps. 12:6 NLT

Let us hold fast the confession
of our hope without wavering,
for He who promised is faithful.
Heb. 10:23 ESV

"I will give them My message, and
what I say will certainly happen...
I, the LORD, make this promise."
Ezek. 12:25 CEV

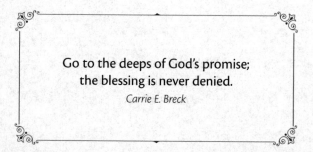

Go to the deeps of God's promise;
the blessing is never denied.

Carrie E. Breck

God always keeps His promises.
Num. 23:19 CEV

I praise God for what He has promised.
I trust in God, so why should I be afraid?
What can mere mortals do to me?
Ps. 56:4 NLT

"I will not violate My covenant
or alter what My lips have uttered."
Ps. 89:34 NIV

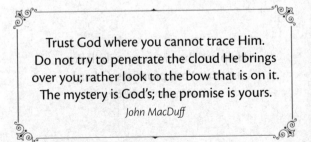

Trust God where you cannot trace Him.
Do not try to penetrate the cloud He brings
over you; rather look to the bow that is on it.
The mystery is God's; the promise is yours.

John MacDuff

*We must never forget His
agreement and His promises,
not in thousands of years.
God made an eternal promise.*
1 Chron. 16:15-16 CEV

*Because of His glory and excellence, He has
given us great and precious promises. These
are the promises that enable you to share
His divine nature and escape the world's
corruption caused by human desires.*
2 Pet. 1:4 NIV

God is able to do whatever He promises.
Rom. 4:21 NLT

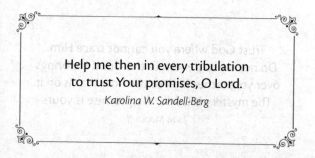

Help me then in every tribulation
to trust Your promises, O Lord.
Karolina W. Sandell-Berg

*He will cover you with His feathers, and
under His wings you will find refuge; His
faithfulness will be your shield and rampart.*

Ps. 91:4 NIV

*He is the Maker of heaven and earth, the sea, and
everything in them – He remains faithful forever.*

Ps. 146:6 NIV

*Sovereign LORD, You are God!
Your covenant is trustworthy.*

2 Sam. 7:28 NIV

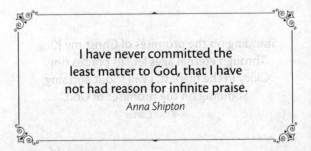

I have never committed the
least matter to God, that I have
not had reason for infinite praise.

Anna Shipton

The LORD is always kind to those who worship Him,
and He keeps His promises to their descendants.
Ps. 103:17 CEV

The Lord is not slow to fulfill His promise as some
count slowness, but is patient toward you.
2 Pet 3:9 ESV

The faithful love of the LORD never ends!
His mercies never cease. Great is His faithfulness;
His mercies begin afresh each morning.
Lam. 3:22-23 NLT

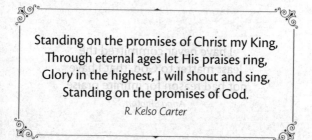

Standing on the promises of Christ my King,
Through eternal ages let His praises ring,
Glory in the highest, I will shout and sing,
Standing on the promises of God.

R. Kelso Carter

God cannot tell lies! And so His promises and
vows are two things that can never be changed.
Heb. 6:18 CEV

Jesus Christ is the same
yesterday and today and forever.
Heb. 13:8 ESV

Your faithfulness extends to every generation,
as enduring as the earth you created.
Ps. 119:90 NLT

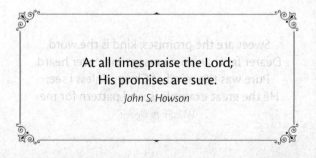

At all times praise the Lord;
His promises are sure.
John S. Howson

The LORD always keeps His promises;
He is gracious in all He does.

Ps. 145:13 NLT

But you, O Lord, are a God merciful and gracious ...
abounding in steadfast love and faithfulness.

Ps. 86:15 ESV

It is by grace you have been saved, through faith –
and this not from yourselves, it is the gift of God.

Eph. 2:8 NIV

Sweet are the promises, kind is the word,
Dearer far than any message man ever heard.
Pure was the mind of Christ, sinless I see;
He the great example is, and pattern for me.

William A. Ogden

Trust in the LORD.

Ps. 4:5 NIV

Fearing people is a dangerous trap,
but trusting the LORD means safety.

Prov. 29:25 NLT

In all your ways acknowledge Him,
and He will make straight your paths.

Prov. 3:6 ESV

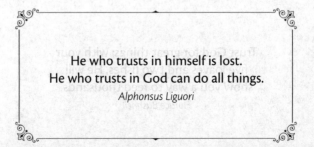

He who trusts in himself is lost.
He who trusts in God can do all things.

Alphonsus Liguori

"Don't let your hearts be troubled. Trust in God."
John 14:1 NLT

May the LORD answer you when you are in distress;
may the name of the God of Jacob protect you.
Ps. 20:1 NIV

Trust the LORD and live right!
The land will be yours,
and you will be safe.
Ps. 37:3 CEV

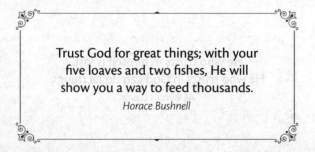

Trust God for great things; with your
five loaves and two fishes, He will
show you a way to feed thousands.
Horace Bushnell

The Scriptures tell us,
"Anyone who trusts in Him
will never be disgraced."

Rom. 10:11 NLT

I have trusted in Your steadfast love;
my heart shall rejoice in Your salvation.

Ps. 13:5 ESV

"I am the LORD All-Powerful,
and I never change."

Mal. 3:6 CEV

I need Thee every hour; teach me Thy will;
And Thy rich promises in me fulfill.

Annie S. Hawks

You bless all of those who trust You, Lord.

Ps. 40:4 CEV

Submit to God and be at peace with Him;
in this way prosperity will come to you.

Job 22:21 NIV

Your unfailing love, O Lord, is as vast as the heavens;
your faithfulness reaches beyond the clouds.

Ps. 36:5 NLT

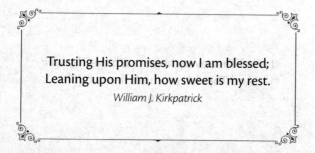

Trusting His promises, now I am blessed;
Leaning upon Him, how sweet is my rest.

William J. Kirkpatrick

Trust in Him at all times. Pour out your
heart to Him, for God is our refuge.

Ps. 62:8 NLT

When I am in distress, I call to You,
because You answer me.

Ps. 86:7 NIV

Everyone who trusts the LORD is like Mount Zion
that cannot be shaken and will stand forever.

Ps. 125:1 CEV

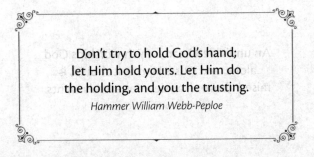

Don't try to hold God's hand;
let Him hold yours. Let Him do
the holding, and you the trusting.

Hammer William Webb-Peploe

*The LORD is good. He protects those
who trust Him in times of trouble.*
Nah. 1:7 CEV

*Those who listen to instruction will prosper;
those who trust the LORD will be joyful.*
Prov. 16:20 NLT

*Be strong and courageous. Do not be frightened,
and do not be dismayed, for the LORD
your God is with you wherever you go.*
Josh. 1:9 ESV

An undivided heart, which worships God
alone, and trusts Him as it should, is
raised above all anxiety for earthly wants.
John Cunningham Geikie

*Those who know Your name put
their trust in You, for You, O Lord,
have not forsaken those who seek You.*
Ps. 9:10 ESV

*The Lord can be trusted to make
you strong and protect you from harm.*
2 Thess. 3:3 CEV

*The Lord is my strength and my shield;
my heart trusts in Him, and He helps me.*
Ps. 28:7 NIV

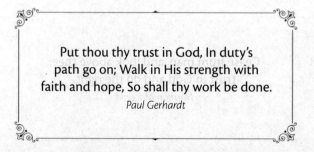

Put thou thy trust in God, In duty's
path go on; Walk in His strength with
faith and hope, So shall thy work be done.

Paul Gerhardt

Let me hear in the morning of Your steadfast
love, for in You I trust. Make me know the
way I should go, for to You I lift up my soul.

Ps. 143:8 ESV

"Don't be afraid. Just have faith."

Mark 5:36 NLT

"Take courage! It is I. Don't be afraid."

Matt. 14:27 NIV

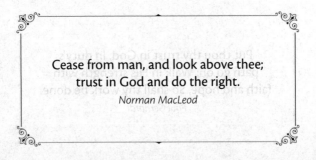

Cease from man, and look above thee;
trust in God and do the right.

Norman MacLeod

I have trusted You without doubting.
Ps. 26:1 CEV

I will put my trust in Him.
Heb. 2:13 NIV

Those who know Your name put
their trust in You, for You, O LORD,
have not forsaken those who seek You.
Ps. 9:10 ESV

The Lord is glorious and strong,
Our God is very high; O trust
in Him, trust now in Him,
And have security.

Thomas T. Lynch

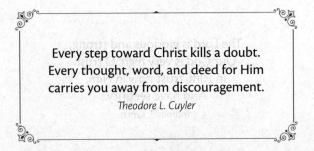

When doubts filled my mind, Your
comfort gave me renewed hope and cheer.
Ps. 94:19 NLT

Bad news won't bother them;
they have decided to trust the LORD.
Ps. 112:7 CEV

Trust in the LORD, and do good;
dwell in the land and befriend faithfulness.
Ps. 37:3 ESV

Every step toward Christ kills a doubt.
Every thought, word, and deed for Him
carries you away from discouragement.
Theodore L. Cuyler

Everything You do is marvelous!
Of this I have no doubt.

Ps. 139:14 CEV

And without faith it is impossible to please Him,
for whoever would draw near to God must believe
that He exists and that He rewards those who seek Him.

Heb. 11:6 ESV

Give your burdens to the LORD, and
He will take care of you. He will not
permit the godly to slip and fall.

Ps. 55:22 NLT

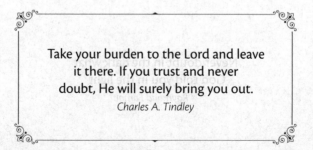

Take your burden to the Lord and leave
it there. If you trust and never
doubt, He will surely bring you out.

Charles A. Tindley

"If you have faith in God and don't doubt,
you can tell this mountain to get up
and jump into the sea, and it will."
Mark 11:23 CEV

Faith is confidence in what we hope for
and assurance about what we do not see.
Heb. 11:1 NIV

For we walk by faith, not by sight.
2 Cor. 5:7 ESV

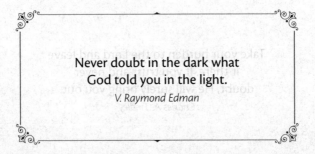

**Never doubt in the dark what
God told you in the light.**
V. Raymond Edman

Seek help from the LORD.

Isa. 31:1 NIV

I am trusting You, O LORD,
saying, "You are my God!"
My future is in Your hands.

Ps. 31:14-15 NLT

LORD, You are my fortress,
my place of safety.

Ps. 91:2 CEV

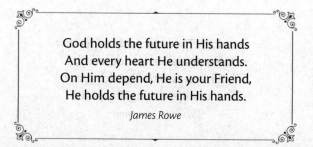

God holds the future in His hands
And every heart He understands.
On Him depend, He is your Friend,
He holds the future in His hands.

James Rowe

"What am I waiting for?
I depend on You, Lord!"

Ps. 39:7 CEV

They all depend on You to give them food
as they need it. When You supply it, they
gather it. You open Your hand to
feed them, and they are richly satisfied.

Ps. 104:27-28 NLT

Be on your guard; stand firm in
the faith; be courageous; be strong.

1 Cor. 16:13 NIV

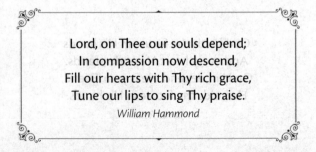

Lord, on Thee our souls depend;
In compassion now descend,
Fill our hearts with Thy rich grace,
Tune our lips to sing Thy praise.

William Hammond

*Trust in the L*ORD *with all your heart;*
do not depend on your own understanding.

Prov. 3:5 NLT

The hope of the righteous brings joy.

Prov. 10:28 ESV

*So always trust the L*ORD *because*
He is forever our mighty rock.

Isa. 26:4 CEV

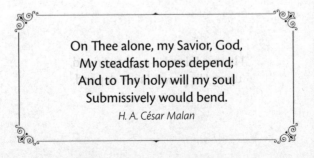

On Thee alone, my Savior, God,
My steadfast hopes depend;
And to Thy holy will my soul
Submissively would bend.

H. A. César Malan

*Deep in my heart I say, "The L*ORD
is all I need; I can depend on Him!"
Lam. 3:24 CEV

*I pray that God, the source of hope, will fill you
completely with joy and peace because you trust
in Him. Then you will overflow with confident
hope through the power of the Holy Spirit.*
Rom. 15:13 NLT

*For You have been my hope, Sovereign L*ORD,
my confidence since my youth.
Ps. 71:5 NIV

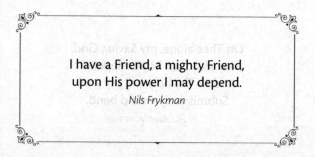

I have a Friend, a mighty Friend,
upon His power I may depend.
Nils Frykman

Only God gives inward peace,
and I depend on Him.
Ps. 62:5 CEV

Since we have been justified through faith, we have
peace with God through our Lord Jesus Christ.
Rom. 5:1 NIV

"The Spirit alone gives eternal life.
Human effort accomplishes nothing.
And the very words I have spoken
to you are spirit and life."
John 6:63 NLT

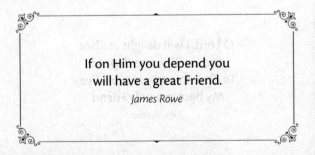

If on Him you depend you
will have a great Friend.
James Rowe

So return to your God.
Patiently trust Him,
and show love and justice.

Hos. 12:6 CEV

The LORD is good to those who depend
on Him, to those who search for Him.

Lam. 3:25 NLT

He brought me out into a broad place;
He rescued me, because He delighted in me.

Ps. 18:19 ESV

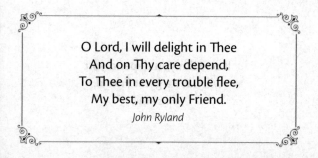

O Lord, I will delight in Thee
And on Thy care depend,
To Thee in every trouble flee,
My best, my only Friend.

John Ryland

He remembers His covenant forever,
the word that He commanded,
for a thousand generations.

Ps. 105:8 ESV

The LORD is righteous in all His
ways and faithful in all He does.

Ps. 145:17 NIV

We don't look at the troubles we can see now; rather,
we fix our gaze on things that cannot be seen.
For the things we see now will soon be gone,
but the things we cannot see will last forever.

2 Cor. 4:18 NLT

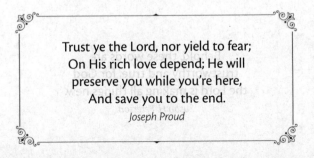

Trust ye the Lord, nor yield to fear;
On His rich love depend; He will
preserve you while you're here,
And save you to the end.

Joseph Proud

Your decrees are very trustworthy; holiness
befits Your house, O LORD, forevermore.
Ps. 93:5 ESV

No one is holy like the LORD!
There is no one besides You;
there is no Rock like our God.
1 Sam. 2:2 NLT

Worship the LORD in the splendor of His
holiness; tremble before Him, all the earth.
Ps. 96:9 NIV

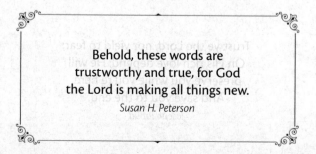

Behold, these words are
trustworthy and true, for God
the Lord is making all things new.
Susan H. Peterson

Our holy God lives forever in the highest heavens,
and this is what He says, "Though I live high
above in the holy place, I am here to help those
who are humble and depend only on Me."

Isa. 57:15 CEV

But You, LORD, are a shield around me,
my glory, the One who lifts my head high.
I call out to the LORD, and He
answers me from His holy mountain.

Ps. 3:3-4 NIV

Strive for peace with everyone,
and for the holiness without which
no one will see the Lord.

Heb. 12:14 ESV

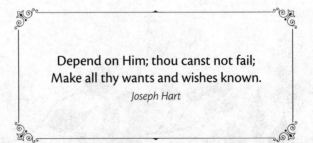

Depend on Him; thou canst not fail;
Make all thy wants and wishes known.

Joseph Hart

November

God will always lead you and
His Word will guide your life.

Jesus said: "I am the light of the world. If you follow Me, you won't have to walk in darkness, because you will have the Light that leads to life."

John 8:12 NLT

God is our God for ever and ever;
He will be our guide even to the end.

Ps. 48:14 NIV

The steps of a man are established by
the LORD, when he delights in His way.

Ps. 37:23 ESV

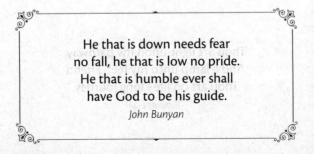

He that is down needs fear
no fall, he that is low no pride.
He that is humble ever shall
have God to be his guide.

John Bunyan

The Lord will guide you always; He will satisfy your needs in a sun-scorched land and will strengthen your frame. You will be like a well-watered garden, like a spring whose waters never fail.

Isa. 58:11 NIV

The instructions of the LORD are perfect, reviving the soul. The decrees of the LORD are trustworthy, making wise the simple.

Ps. 19:7 NLT

Make me to know Your ways, O LORD; teach me Your paths. Lead me in Your truth and teach me, for You are the God of my salvation; for You I wait all the day long.

Ps. 25:4-5 ESV

Thou art light upon my pathway,
And a lamp unto my feet; Friend
Thou art on life's long journey.

Thomas Levi

The LORD says, "I will guide you along
the best pathway for your life.
I will advise you and watch over you."

Ps. 32:8-9 NLT

Thus says the LORD, your Redeemer, the Holy One
of Israel: "I am the LORD your God, who teaches you to
profit, who leads you in the way you should go."

Isa. 48:17 ESV

The LORD replied, "My Presence will
go with you, and I will give you rest."

Exod. 33:14 NIV

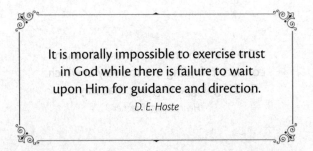

It is morally impossible to exercise trust
in God while there is failure to wait
upon Him for guidance and direction.

D. E. Hoste

Without guidance from God law and order disappear,
but God blesses everyone who obeys His Law.
Prov. 29:18 CEV

All who are led by the Spirit of God are children of God.
Rom. 8:14 NLT

Show me Your ways, LORD, teach me Your paths.
Guide me in Your truth and teach me, for You are
God my Savior, and my hope is in You all day long.
Ps. 25:4-5 NIV

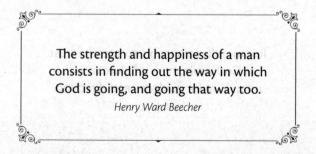

The strength and happiness of a man
consists in finding out the way in which
God is going, and going that way too.

Henry Ward Beecher

*God hid them under a cloud and
guided them by fire during the night.*
Ps. 105:39 CEV

*"I will go before you and will level the
mountains; I will break down gates
of bronze and cut through bars of iron."*
Isa. 45:2 NIV

*The lot is cast into the lap, but its
every decision is from the LORD.*
Prov. 16:33 ESV

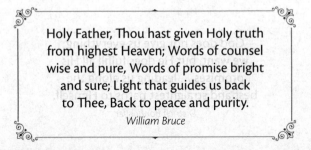

Holy Father, Thou hast given Holy truth
from highest Heaven; Words of counsel
wise and pure, Words of promise bright
and sure; Light that guides us back
to Thee, Back to peace and purity.

William Bruce

*The Lamb in the midst of the throne
will be their shepherd, and He will
guide them to springs of living water.*
Rev. 7:17 ESV

*Lead me by Your truth and teach me,
for You are the God who saves me.
All day long I put my hope in You.*
Ps. 25:5 NLT

*Whether you turn to the right or to the left,
your ears will hear a voice behind you,
saying, "This is the way; walk in it."*
Isa. 30:21 NIV

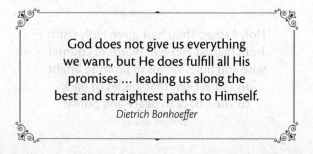

God does not give us everything
we want, but He does fulfill all His
promises … leading us along the
best and straightest paths to Himself.
Dietrich Bonhoeffer

*The Lord's Word is a lamp to my
feet and a light to my path.*

Ps. 119:105 ESV

*"Even more blessed are all who hear
the word of God and put it into practice."*

Luke 11:28 NLT

*"The grass withers and the flowers fall,
but the word of our God endures forever."*

Isa. 40:8 NIV

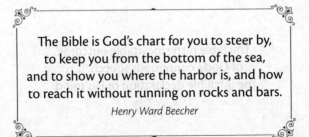

The Bible is God's chart for you to steer by,
to keep you from the bottom of the sea,
and to show you where the harbor is, and how
to reach it without running on rocks and bars.

Henry Ward Beecher

Everything in the Scriptures is God's Word.
All of it is useful for teaching and helping people
and for correcting them and showing them how to live.

2 Tim. 3:16 CEV

Study this Book of Instruction continually.
Meditate on it day and night so you will be
sure to obey everything written in it. Only
then will you prosper and succeed in all you do.

Josh. 1:8 NLT

For the word of the LORD is right
and true; He is faithful in all He does.

Ps. 33:4 NIV

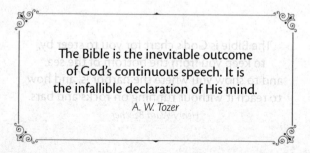

The Bible is the inevitable outcome
of God's continuous speech. It is
the infallible declaration of His mind.

A. W. Tozer

Don't just listen to God's Word.
You must do what it says.
James 1:22 NLT

Everything that was written in the
past was written to teach us, so that
through the endurance taught in
the Scriptures and the encouragement
they provide we might have hope.
Rom. 15:4 NIV

For the word of the LORD is upright,
and all His work is done in faithfulness.
Ps. 33:4 ESV

Happy is the soul which by a sincere
self-renunciation, holds itself ceaselessly in the
hands of its Creator, ready to do everything
which He wishes; which never stops
saying to itself a hundred times a day,
"Lord, what would You have me do?"

François Fénelon

*The Son is the radiance of God's glory
and the exact representation of His being,
sustaining all things by His powerful Word.*
Heb. 1:3 NIV

*The LORD is good and does what is right;
He shows the proper path to those who go astray.*
Ps. 25:8 NLT

*The unfolding of Your words gives light;
it imparts understanding to the simple.*
Ps. 119:130 ESV

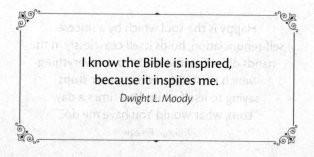

I know the Bible is inspired,
because it inspires me.

Dwight L. Moody

*Those who obey God's word truly
show how completely they love Him.*
1 John 2:5 NLT

*How can a young man keep his way pure?
By guarding it according to Your word.*
Ps. 119:9 ESV

*May the Lord direct your hearts into
God's love and Christ's perseverance.*
2 Thess. 3:5 NIV

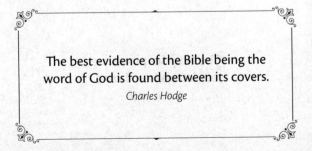

The best evidence of the Bible being the
word of God is found between its covers.

Charles Hodge

As for God, His way is perfect:
The LORD's Word is flawless; He
shields all who take refuge in Him.

Ps. 18:30 NIV

I rejoice at Your word like
one who finds great spoil.

Ps. 119:162 ESV

Guide my steps by Your word,
so I will not be overcome by evil.

Ps. 119:133 NLT

The Holy Scriptures are
our letters from home.

St. Augustine

The LORD our God will lead the way.

Deut. 1:30 CEV

*Where there is no guidance, a people falls, but
in an abundance of counselors there is safety.*

Prov. 11:14 ESV

He will show them the path they should choose.

Ps. 25:12 NLT

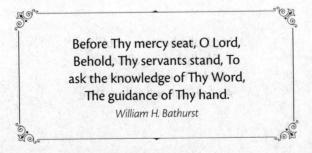

Before Thy mercy seat, O Lord,
Behold, Thy servants stand, To
ask the knowledge of Thy Word,
The guidance of Thy hand.

William H. Bathurst

God is with us; He is our leader.

2 Chron. 13:12 NIV

*But I never really left you, and you hold My
right hand. Your advice has been my guide,
and later You will welcome me in glory.*

Ps. 73:23-24 CEV

*A man's steps are from the LORD;
how then can man understand His way?*

Prov. 20:24 ESV

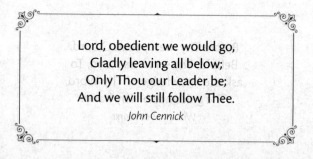

Lord, obedient we would go,
Gladly leaving all below;
Only Thou our Leader be;
And we will still follow Thee.

John Cennick

*"I am the LORD your God, who teaches you to profit,
who leads you in the way you should go."*

Isa. 48:17 ESV

*Send out Your light and Your truth;
let them guide me. Let them
lead me to Your holy mountain,
to the place where You live.*

Ps. 43:3 NLT

*In all your ways submit to Him,
and He will make your paths straight.*

Prov. 3:6 NIV

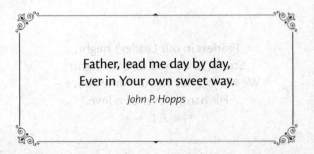

Father, lead me day by day,
Ever in Your own sweet way.

John P. Hopps

The LORD God of Israel will lead and protect you.
Isa. 52:12 CEV

"When the Spirit of truth comes, He will
guide you into all the truth, for He will
not speak on His own authority, but
whatever He hears He will speak, and He
will declare to you the things that are to come."
John 16:13 ESV

"When the Father sends the Advocate as my
representative – that is, the Holy Spirit –
He will teach you everything and will
remind you of everything I have told you."
John 14:26 NLT

Fearless in our Leader's might,
Strong to do and dare the right;
We will journey to our home above –
His banner over us is love.
Helen H. Lemmel

You killed Jesus by nailing Him to a cross.
But the God our ancestors worshiped raised
Him to life and made Him our Leader and Savior.

Acts 5:30-31 CEV

"I am the way, the truth, and the life. No one
can come to the Father except through Me."

John 14:6 NLT

Teach me to do Your will, for You are my God!
Let Your good Spirit lead me on level ground!

Ps. 143:10 ESV

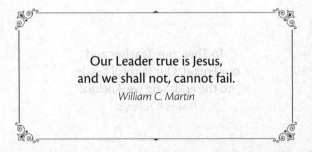

Our Leader true is Jesus,
and we shall not, cannot fail.

William C. Martin

Thanks be to God, who in Christ always
leads us in triumphal procession, and
through us spreads the fragrance of
the knowledge of Him everywhere.

2 Cor. 2:14 ESV

"Do not defile yourselves by turning to
mediums or to those who consult the spirits
of the dead. I am the LORD your God."

Lev. 19:31 NLT

He lifted me out of the slimy pit,
out of the mud and mire;
He set my feet on a rock and
gave me a firm place to stand.

Ps. 40:2 NIV

To Thee, our Teacher and
our Friend, Our faithful Leader
to the end, Sing we Alleluia!

Frances R. Havergal

Be humble when you correct people who oppose you. Maybe God will lead them to turn to Him and learn the truth.

2 Tim. 2:25 CEV

Blessed is the man whom you discipline, O LORD, and whom you teach out of Your law, to give him rest from days of trouble, until a pit is dug for the wicked. For the LORD will not forsake His people; He will not abandon His heritage.

Ps. 94:12-14 ESV

Teach me to do your will, for you are my God. May your gracious Spirit lead me forward on a firm footing.

Ps. 143:10 NLT

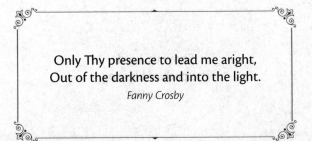

Only Thy presence to lead me aright,
Out of the darkness and into the light.

Fanny Crosby

God, for whom and through whom
everything was made, chose to bring
many children into glory. And it was
only right that He should make Jesus,
through His suffering, a perfect leader,
fit to bring them into their salvation.

Heb. 2:10 NLT

You know when I sit down and when I rise up;
You discern my thoughts from afar.

Ps. 139:2 ESV

Lead me, LORD, in Your righteousness
because of my enemies –
make Your way straight before me.

Ps. 5:8 NIV

Show us, Lord,
the path of blessing.
Heinrich Held

*Jesus is forever able to save
the people He leads to God.*
Heb. 7:25 CEV

*O LORD, You have searched
me and known me!*
Ps. 139:1 ESV

*"Whoever serves Me must follow Me; and
where I am, My servant also will be.
My Father will honor the one who serves Me."*
John 12:26 NIV

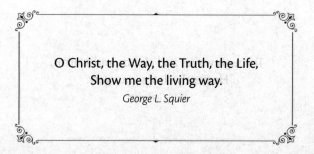

O Christ, the Way, the Truth, the Life,
Show me the living way.
George L. Squier

*We must keep our eyes on Jesus, who
leads us and makes our faith complete.*

Heb. 12:2 CEV

*Don't act thoughtlessly, but understand
what the Lord wants you to do.*

Eph. 5:17 NLT

*For with You is the fountain of life;
in Your light do we see light.*

Ps. 36:9 ESV

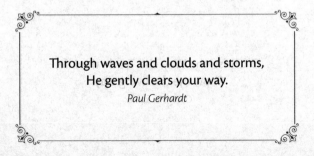

Through waves and clouds and storms,
He gently clears your way.

Paul Gerhardt

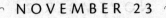

When Christ did come, it was to
lead you to have faith in God.
1 Pet. 1:21 CEV

He restores my soul. He leads me in
paths of righteousness for His name's sake.
Ps. 23:3 ESV

Faith comes from hearing the
message, and the message is heard
through the word about Christ
Rom. 10:17 NIV

Lead us by faith to hope's
true promised land;
be Thou our Guide.
Hugh T. Kerr

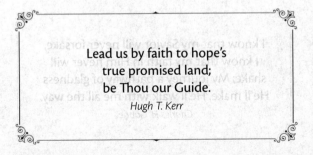

The LORD will lead you into the land.
He will always be with you and
help you, so don't ever be afraid.

Deut. 31:8 CEV

I sought the LORD, and He answered
me and delivered me from all my fears.

Ps. 34:4 ESV

"I am the light of the world. Whoever
follows Me will never walk in darkness,
but will have the light of life."

John 8:12 NIV

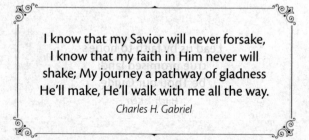

I know that my Savior will never forsake,
I know that my faith in Him never will
shake; My journey a pathway of gladness
He'll make, He'll walk with me all the way.

Charles H. Gabriel

"I am the Lord, and I lead you along the right path.
If you obey Me, we will walk together."

Hos. 14:9 CEV

You shall walk in all the way that the
LORD your God has commanded you,
that you may live, and that it may go well
with you, and that you may live long in
the land that you shall possess.

Deut. 5:33 ESV

Anyone who remains in the teaching
of Christ has a relationship with
both the Father and the Son.

2 John 1:9 NLT

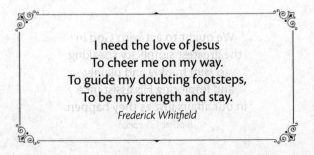

I need the love of Jesus
To cheer me on my way.
To guide my doubting footsteps,
To be my strength and stay.

Frederick Whitfield

The LORD Himself will guide you.

Mic. 2:13 NLT

*You, LORD God, are my mighty rock
and my fortress. Lead me and guide me,
so that Your name will be honored.*

Ps. 31:3 CEV

*Teach me Your way, O LORD,
that I may walk in Your truth.*

Ps. 86:11 ESV

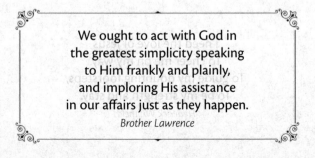

We ought to act with God in
the greatest simplicity speaking
to Him frankly and plainly,
and imploring His assistance
in our affairs just as they happen.

Brother Lawrence

"Truly, I say to you, whoever hears My Word
and believes Him who sent Me has eternal life."

John 5:24 ESV

For the word of God is alive and active.
Sharper than any double-edged sword,
it penetrates even to dividing soul and spirit,
joints and marrow; it judges the
thoughts and attitudes of the heart.

Heb. 4:12 NIV

The LORD's instruction is right; it makes our hearts glad.
His commands shine brightly, and they give us light.

Ps. 19:8 CEV

It is necessary to apply Scripture in
order to learn the sure marks which
distinguish God, as Creator of the world,
from the whole herd of fictitious gods.

John Calvin

You have shown me the way of life, Lord, and
You will fill me with the joy of Your presence.

Acts 2:28 NLT

You make known to me the path of life;
in Your presence there is fullness of joy.

Ps.16:11 ESV

Lead me to the rock that is higher than I.

Ps. 61:2 NIV

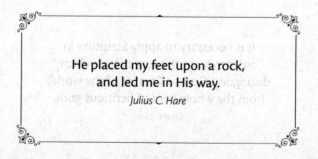

He placed my feet upon a rock,
and led me in His way.

Julius C. Hare

When you are tempted, God will show
you a way out so that you can endure.
1 Cor. 10:13 NLT

Submit to God and be at peace with Him;
in this way prosperity will come to you.
Job 22:21 NIV

Therefore, as you received
Christ Jesus the Lord, so walk in Him.
Col. 2:6 ESV

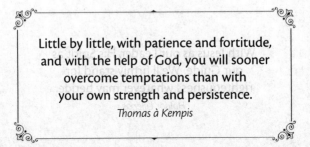

Little by little, with patience and fortitude,
and with the help of God, you will sooner
overcome temptations than with
your own strength and persistence.

Thomas à Kempis

*He guides the humble in what is
right and teaches them His way.*
Ps. 25:9 NIV

*Teach me how to live, O LORD.
Lead me along the right path.*
Ps. 27:11 NLT

*Teach me ... make me understand
how I have gone astray.*
Job 6:24 ESV

With Jesus as our Leader, His Spirit as
our Guide, We'll firmly stand for
righteousness whatever may betide.

Haldor Lillenas

December

God is a patient, forgiving and kind God.

*If we confess our sins to God, He can always
be trusted to forgive us and take our sins away.*

1 John 1:9 CEV

*"I will forgive their wickedness, and I
will never again remember their sins."*

Heb. 8:12 NLT

*I acknowledged my sin to You, and I did
not cover my iniquity; I said, "I will
confess my transgressions to the LORD,"
and You forgave the iniquity of my sin. Selah*

Ps. 32:5 ESV

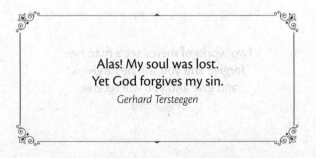

Alas! My soul was lost.
Yet God forgives my sin.

Gerhard Tersteegen

The Lord our God is merciful and forgiving.

Dan. 9:9 NLT

*"If you forgive others for the wrongs they do to you,
your Father in heaven will forgive you."*

Matt. 6:14 CEV

Forgive as the Lord forgave you.

Col. 3:13 NIV

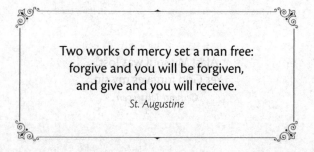

Two works of mercy set a man free:
forgive and you will be forgiven,
and give and you will receive.

St. Augustine

"Come now, let us settle the matter," says
the LORD. "Though your sins are like scarlet,
they shall be as white as snow; though they
are red as crimson, they shall be like wool."

Isa. 1:18 NIV

"I have rescued you and swept away
your sins as though they were clouds."

Isa. 44:22 CEV

He has delivered us from the domain of darkness and
transferred us to the kingdom of His beloved Son,
in whom we have redemption, the forgiveness of sins.

Col. 1:13-14 ESV

Our faults and failings He forgives;
His mercies – who can tell!

William M. Runyan

*As far as the east is from the west, so far does
the LORD remove our transgressions from us.*

Ps. 103:12 ESV

*Who is a God like You, who pardons sin and forgives
the transgression of the remnant of His inheritance?
You do not stay angry forever but delight to
show mercy. You will again have compassion
on us; You will tread our sins underfoot and
hurl all our iniquities into the depths of the sea.*

Mic. 7:18-19 NIV

*Because you belong to Him, the power
of the life-giving Spirit has freed you
from the power of sin that leads to death.*

Rom. 8:2 NLT

God has cast our confessed sins into
the depths of the sea, and He's even
put a "No Fishing" sign over the spot.

Dwight L. Moody

You are a God ready to forgive,
gracious and merciful.

Neh. 9:17 ESV

The LORD is good to everyone. He showers
compassion on all His creation.

Ps. 145:9 NLT

God was merciful! We were dead because
of our sins, but God loved us so much
that He made us alive with Christ, and
God's wonderful kindness is what saves you.

Eph. 2:4-5 CEV

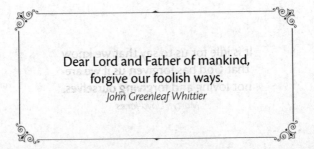

Dear Lord and Father of mankind,
forgive our foolish ways.

John Greenleaf Whittier

The LORD is slow to anger and
abounding in steadfast love,
forgiving iniquity and transgression.

Num. 14:18 ESV

But if anyone does sin, we have an advocate
who pleads our case before the Father.
He is Jesus Christ, the One who is truly righteous.
He himself is the sacrifice that atones for our sins –
and not only our sins but the sins of all the world.

1 John 2:1-2 NLT

Everyone who believes in Him receives
forgiveness of sins through His name.

Acts 10:43 NIV

It is idle for us to say that we know
that God has forgiven us if we are
not loving and forgiving ourselves.
Martyn Lloyd-Jones

The LORD is merciful! He is kind and patient, and His love never fails.

Ps. 103:8 CEV

For His unfailing love for us is powerful; the LORD's faithfulness endures forever.

Ps. 117:2 NLT

In everything we do, we show that we are true ministers of God. We patiently endure troubles and hardships and calamities of every kind.

2 Cor. 6:4 NLT

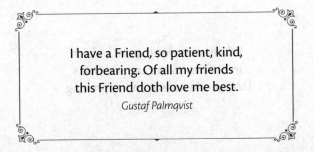

I have a Friend, so patient, kind, forbearing. Of all my friends this Friend doth love me best.

Gustaf Palmqvist

The LORD is powerful, yet patient.
Nah. 1:3 CEV

The Lord is not slow in keeping His promise,
as some understand slowness.
Instead He is patient with you.
2 Pet. 3:9 NIV

Be still in the presence of the LORD,
and wait patiently for Him to act.
Ps. 37:7 NLT

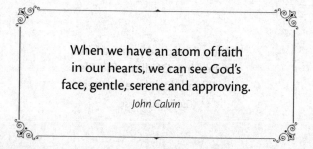

When we have an atom of faith
in our hearts, we can see God's
face, gentle, serene and approving.
John Calvin

*"I am the LORD God. I am merciful
and very patient with My people."*

Exod. 34:6 CEV

*The LORD is good to those who wait
for Him, to the soul who seeks Him.*

Lam. 3:25 NIV

*They who wait for the LORD shall renew
their strength; they shall mount up with
wings like eagles; they shall run and not
be weary; they shall walk and not faint.*

Isa. 40:31 ESV

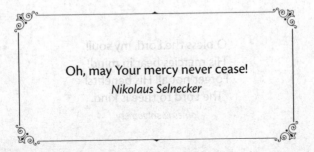

Oh, may Your mercy never cease!
Nikolaus Selnecker

LORD, You have always been patient and kind.

Ps. 25:6 CEV

Wait for the LORD; be strong and
take heart and wait for the LORD.

Ps. 27:14 NIV

How precious is Your steadfast love, O God!

Ps. 36:7 ESV

O bless the Lord, my soul!
His mercies bear in mind!
Forget not all His benefits!
The Lord to thee is kind.

James Montgomery

You know that you learn to endure by having your faith tested. But you must learn to endure everything, so that you will be completely mature and not lacking in anything.

James 1:3-4 CEV

Let us then with confidence draw near to the throne of grace, that we may receive mercy and find grace to help in time of need.

Heb. 4:16 ESV

You need to persevere so that when you have done the will of God, you will receive what He has promised.

Heb. 10:36 NIV

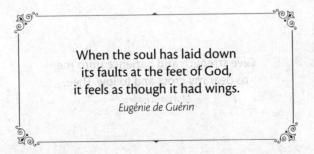

When the soul has laid down
its faults at the feet of God,
it feels as though it had wings.

Eugénie de Guérin

*Don't forget that the Lord is patient
because He wants people to be saved.*
2 Pet. 3:15 CEV

*So it is good to wait quietly
for salvation from the LORD.*
Lam. 3:26 NLT

*May the Lord direct your hearts into
God's love and Christ's perseverance.*
2 Thess. 3:5 NIV

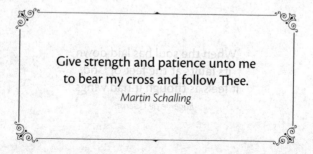

Give strength and patience unto me
to bear my cross and follow Thee.
Martin Schalling

Have mercy on me, O God, because of Your
unfailing love. Because of Your great
compassion, blot out the stain of my sins.
Purify me from my sins, and I will be clean;
wash me, and I will be whiter than snow.

Ps. 51:1, 7 NLT

You, Lord, are forgiving and good,
abounding in love to all who call to You.

Ps. 86:5 NIV

My friends, the message is that
Jesus can forgive your sins!

Acts 13:38 CEV

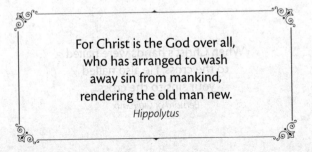

For Christ is the God over all,
who has arranged to wash
away sin from mankind,
rendering the old man new.

Hippolytus

God our Savior saved us, not because of the righteous
things we had done, but because of His mercy.
He washed away our sins, giving us a new birth
and new life through the Holy Spirit.

Titus 3:5 NLT

So Christ was sacrificed once to take away
the sins of many; and He will appear a
second time, not to bear sin, but to bring
salvation to those who are waiting for Him.

Heb. 9:28 NIV

In Him we have redemption through His
blood, the forgiveness of our trespasses,
according to the riches of His grace.

Eph. 1:7 ESV

When Christ's hands were nailed
to the cross, He also nailed
your sins to the cross.

Bernard of Clairvaux

If we live in the light, as God does,
we share in life with each other.
And the blood of His Son Jesus
washes all our sins away.

1 John 1:7 CEV

Repent, then, and turn to God, so that
your sins may be wiped out, that times
of refreshing may come from the Lord.

Acts 3:19 NIV

Let Your mercy come to me, that I
may live; for Your law is my delight.

Ps. 119:77 ESV

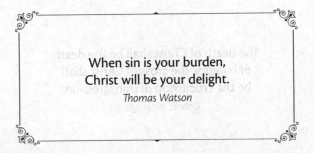

When sin is your burden,
Christ will be your delight.

Thomas Watson

Let us strip off every weight that slows us down,
especially the sin that so easily trips us up.
And let us run with endurance the race God has set
before us. We do this by keeping our eyes on Jesus,
the champion who initiates and perfects our faith.

Heb. 12:1-2 NLT

He took a cup, and when He had given thanks
He gave it to them, saying, "Drink of it, all of you,
for this is My blood of the covenant, which is
poured out for many for the forgiveness of sins."

Matt. 26:27-28 ESV

Direct my footsteps according to
Your Word; let no sin rule over me.

Ps. 119:133 NIV

The death of Christ shall be the death
of iniquity, the cross of Christ shall
be the crucifixion of transgression.

Charles H. Spurgeon

Don't you see how wonderfully kind,
tolerant, and patient God is with you?
Rom. 2:4 NLT

Let them give thanks to the LORD for His unfailing
love and His wonderful deeds for mankind.
Ps. 107:8 NIV

The LORD takes pleasure in those who fear Him,
in those who hope in His steadfast love.
Ps. 147:11 ESV

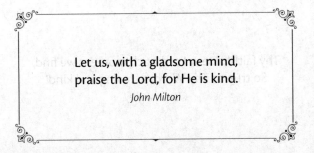

Let us, with a gladsome mind,
praise the Lord, for He is kind.
John Milton

Shout praises to the LORD! Our God is kind,
and it is right and good to sing praises to Him.
Ps. 147:1 CEV

We praise God for the glorious grace He has
poured out on us who belong to His dear Son.
He is so rich in kindness and grace
that He purchased our freedom with
the blood of His Son and forgave our sins.
Eph. 1:6-7 NLT

You are good, and what You do
is good; teach me Your decrees.
Ps. 119:68 NIV

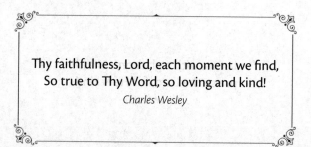

Thy faithfulness, Lord, each moment we find,
So true to Thy Word, so loving and kind!
Charles Wesley

*I have talked about Your faithfulness and saving
power. I have told everyone in the great
assembly of Your unfailing love and faithfulness.*
Ps. 40:10 NLT

You are kind and good ... You are truly merciful.
Ps. 69:16 CEV

*For the LORD is good and His love endures forever;
His faithfulness continues through all generations.*
Ps. 100:5 NIV

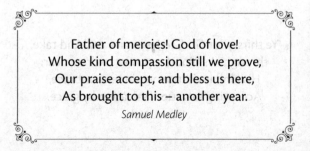

Father of mercies! God of love!
Whose kind compassion still we prove,
Our praise accept, and bless us here,
As brought to this – another year.

Samuel Medley

The Lord is kind, and as soon as He
hears your cries for help, He will come.
Isa. 30:19 CEV

I waited patiently for the LORD;
He turned to me and heard my cry.
Ps. 40:1 NIV

The LORD is good! Blessed is the
man who takes refuge in Him!
Ps. 34:8 ESV

Ye thirsty for God, to Jesus give ear, And take,
through His blood, a power to draw near;
His kind invitation ye sinners embrace,
Accepting salvation, salvation by grace.
Charles Wesley

~ DECEMBER 21 ~

The Lord loves justice and fairness, and
He is kind to everyone everywhere on earth.
Ps. 33:5 CEV

I remain confident of this:
I will see the goodness of the LORD
in the land of the living.
Ps. 27:13 NIV

They shall pour forth the fame of
Your abundant goodness and shall
sing aloud of Your righteousness.
Ps. 145:7 ESV

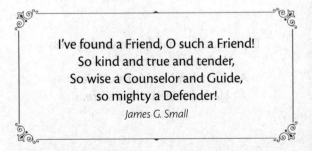

I've found a Friend, O such a Friend!
So kind and true and tender,
So wise a Counselor and Guide,
so mighty a Defender!

James G. Small

*Tell the LORD how thankful you are,
because He is kind and always merciful.*
Ps. 118:1 CEV

*Whoever conceals their sins does not
prosper, but the one who confesses and
renounces them finds mercy.*
Prov. 28:13 NIV

*Praise the LORD, for the LORD is good;
celebrate His lovely name.*
Ps. 135:3 NLT

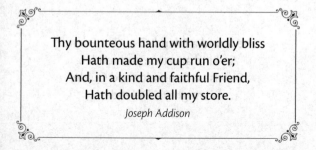

Thy bounteous hand with worldly bliss
Hath made my cup run o'er;
And, in a kind and faithful Friend,
Hath doubled all my store.

Joseph Addison

Praise the name of the LORD!
He is kind and good.
Ps. 135:3 CEV

Oh give thanks to the LORD, for He is good.
Ps. 106:1 ESV

You, Lord, are a compassionate and gracious God,
slow to anger, abounding in love and faithfulness.
Ps. 86:15 NIV

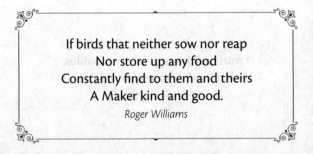

If birds that neither sow nor reap
Nor store up any food
Constantly find to them and theirs
A Maker kind and good.

Roger Williams

The LORD is kind to everyone who is humble.
Prov. 3:34 CEV

*In His kindness God called you to share
in His eternal glory by means of Christ Jesus ...
He will restore, support, and strengthen you,
and He will place you on a firm foundation.*
1 Pet. 5:10 NLT

The grace of the Lord Jesus be with God's people.
Rev. 22:21 NIV

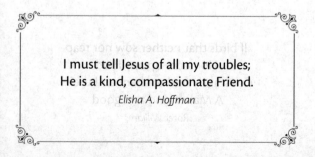

I must tell Jesus of all my troubles;
He is a kind, compassionate Friend.
Elisha A. Hoffman

God our Father loves us. He is kind and has
given us eternal comfort and a wonderful hope.
2 Thess. 2:16 CEV

Therefore the Lord waits to be gracious to you,
and therefore He exalts Himself to show
mercy to you. For the LORD is a God of justice;
blessed are all those who wait for Him.
Isa. 30:18 ESV

The grace of the Lord Jesus Christ be with your spirit.
Philem. 1:25 ESV

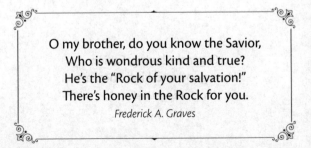

O my brother, do you know the Savior,
Who is wondrous kind and true?
He's the "Rock of your salvation!"
There's honey in the Rock for you.

Frederick A. Graves

*Christ has also introduced us to God's undeserved
kindness on which we take our stand.*

Rom. 5:2 CEV

*For the LORD your God is gracious
and merciful and will not turn away His
face from you, if you return to Him.*

2 Chron. 30:9 ESV

"I will be merciful to you."

Jer. 42:12 NLT

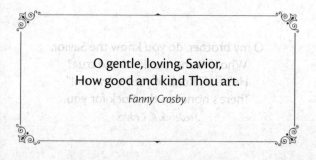

O gentle, loving, Savior,
How good and kind Thou art.

Fanny Crosby

*Jesus Christ alone brought God's
gift of kindness to many people.*
Rom. 5:15 CEV

Show me Your unfailing love in wonderful ways.
Ps. 17:7 NLT

*Full of splendor and majesty is His work, and His
righteousness endures forever. He has caused
His wondrous works to be remembered;
the LORD is gracious and merciful.*
Ps. 111:3-4 ESV

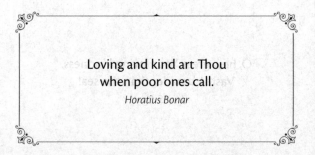

Loving and kind art Thou
when poor ones call.
Horatius Bonar

God was kind! He made me what I am,
and His wonderful kindness wasn't wasted.
1 Cor. 15:10 CEV

He is my loving God and my fortress,
my stronghold and my deliverer,
my shield, in whom I take refuge.
Ps. 144:2 NIV

The LORD is like a father to His children,
tender and compassionate to those who fear Him.
Ps. 103:13 NLT

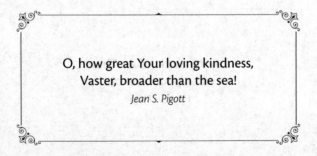

O, how great Your loving kindness,
Vaster, broader than the sea!

Jean S. Pigott

*God will treat you with undeserved
kindness and will bless you with peace.*
Gal. 6:16 CEV

*How kind the LORD is! How good He is!
So merciful, this God of ours!*
Ps. 116:5 NLT

*Your compassion, LORD, is great;
preserve my life according to Your laws.*
Ps. 119:156 NIV

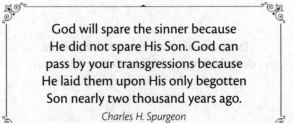

God will spare the sinner because
He did not spare His Son. God can
pass by your transgressions because
He laid them upon His only begotten
Son nearly two thousand years ago.

Charles H. Spurgeon

God has shown us how kind
He is by coming to save all people.
Titus 2:11 CEV

"I have loved you with an everlasting love;
I have drawn you with unfailing kindness."
Jer. 31:3 NIV

Be kind and compassionate to one
another, forgiving each other,
just as in Christ God forgave you.
Eph. 4:32 ESV

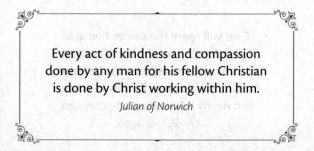

Every act of kindness and compassion
done by any man for his fellow Christian
is done by Christ working within him.

Julian of Norwich

*Make sure that no one misses out
on God's wonderful kindness.*
Heb. 12:15 CEV

*Lord, don't hold back Your tender mercies from me.
Let Your unfailing love and faithfulness always protect me.*
Ps. 40:11 NLT

*We have thought on Your steadfast love,
O God, in the midst of Your temple.*
Ps. 48:9 ESV

Endeavor to be always patient of the faults
and imperfections of others, for thou hast
many faults and imperfections of thy own
that require a reciprocation of forbearance.

Thomas à Kempis